LEN BEADELL

AROUND THE WORLD
IN EIGHTY DELAYS

Also by Len Beadell:
  Too Long in the Bush
  Blast the Bush
  Bush Bashers
  Still in the Bush
  Beating About the Bush
  End of an Era
  Outback Highways (a compilation)

ISBN 1 876247 01 0 (hardback)
ISBN 1 876247 02 9 (paperback)

National Library of Australia
Cataloguing-in-Publication entry:
    Beadell, Len 1923-1995
    AROUND THE WORLD IN EIGHTY DELAYS.
    ISBN 1 876 247 010
    Voyages around the world – Humour. I. Title.
    910.410207

First published by Corkwood Press 1997
Second edition 1998
Copyright © Anne Beadell
Design Copyright © Corkwood Press 1997

Wholly designed and typeset in Australia
by Corkwood Press

Printed in Australia for Corkwood Press
PO Box 237
North Adelaide
South Australia 5006

e-mail corkwood@onaustralia.com.au

CONTENTS

INTRODUCTION

I MET Lennie in 1960, the year after he did his world trip, and we married not long after. In our 34 years together—until he died in 1995—we did many trips overseas and around Australia. It didn't take me long to realise that no trip was complete without calling in on somebody, and we would call in on people wherever possible. Having very much enjoyed the company of the British scientists during the atomic tests and rocket programme of the 40s and 50s, it is logical that Lennie should want to call in on them during his long service leave in 1959. Even more typical is that his visit to England should include the rest of the world, given his propensity to cram in as much as possible on a trip. No leisurely trips for Lennie!

He always liked to have fun, and the Lennie in this book is the man I first met. Being English was greatly in my favour: he was *bound* to like me! He remained throughout his life a simple, gentle and quiet country boy, with an infectious laugh and quirky sense of humour. Lennie was absolutely secure in himself—he thought everybody else was different. Those of us who have enjoyed his humour over the years can picture his astonishment and fascination with the vagaries of the rest of the world. As with Phineas Fogg in Jules Verne's classic *Around the World in Eighty Days*, when Lennie was out of his element, peculiar things happened. Mike Todd's film, starring David Niven, was receiving much publicity at the time of writing, hence Lennie's idea for his title.

This 1959 world tour was a big event in his life. Indeed, it was an unusual and major thing for *anyone* to do in the fifties. When I first met him it was still fresh in his mind; he had loved every moment of it and would regale us with stories from his trips in his inimitable way, poking fun at himself and sending up his image of the simple country boy let loose in the big city.

His one disappointment in a life full of achievement and high points was that *Around the World in Eighty Delays* was never published. Although written with so much enthusiasm in 1967, publishers decided it was too different from the bush books and that the public weren't quite ready for the 'Townie' Lennie. My family and I are absolutely delighted that Richard Barnes and Corkwood Press have agreed to print the book with the original text and drawings just as Lennie envisaged.

To enjoy this book, transport yourself back to the fifties— before the digital revolution and the age of fast travel. Australia was just beginning to see the wisdom of coming out of its isolation and joining the post-war push for prosperity. The leisure 4WD vehicle trend had not yet begun. Desert travel for recreation was rare, and life in the outback, as Lennie lived it, was one of isolation and survival in a most basic fashion. Picture a man removed from a desert wilderness to the razzmatazz of Las Vegas. . .

Anne Beadell,
Williamstown, South Australia,
July 1997.

PUBLISHER'S NOTE

LEN Beadell's hitherto unpublished book has all the charm and gentle wit which is a feature of his other works.

I first saw the original manuscript on a visit to Anne Beadell in May 1997 and realised that it should be published.

As with his other books, Len drew cartoons to go with the text. Some of these, towards the end of the book, remain in the first draft state. However, they have been included as was Len's intention, despite their unpolished appearance. Len took many slides whilst on this journey and it has been a difficult job deciding which should be included. Where possible, I have published those which appear to represent special events referred to in the text.

I would like to thank Anne and Connie Sue Beadell who have unearthed the photographs and illustrations which accompany the text and have advised me at every stage. I'm also grateful to Renata Cirocco, Louise Kruger, and Maureen Carpenter for typing the manuscript. Thanks also to my wife Marie-Lou, who worked tirelessly to correct the final draft and Dr James Cooper for guidance with correction of typographical, spelling and punctuation errors.

The success of the first edition of this book, together with the interest in Mark Shephard's *A Lifetime in the Bush: the biography of Len Beadell*, also published by Corkwood Press, shows Australia's fascination for this great man is alive and well.

Richard Barnes,
Rose Park, South Australia,
March 1998.

Chapter 1

NEVER SAY 'FRISCO

'OPERATOR! I think there is a television set right here in my room.'

'You what?' The girl with the usually bright American accent sounded incredulous.

'I said I think there is a television set right here in my room and I was wondering how to get it to go.'

'Honey! You're kidding...'

'No you see I've just come from Australia and...'

'Why then, of course you really wouldn't know.'

She sounded relieved. I had only just started on this round the world trip after having been camping in Central Australia for most of my life and this was my introduction to San Francisco.

THE long survey programme of our atomic bomb testing ground at Maralinga had been coming to an end and I had been due to resume a series of expeditions into the unknown deserts across Australia, continuing on with my latest projects surveying unexplored parts of the outback. The British team of atomic scientists at the site had been working on me for months along the lines of getting me to make a visit to England, where they would all be returning after the tests. Slowly I had come round to the idea.

There had been a bush field telephone wired to a mulga tree where I was working one morning and the sight of it together with an observation made by a clerk at H.Q. gave me an idea. He had mentioned a few years before that I was due for long service leave. So, leaving my theodolite set up, I padded in my hob-nailed boots through the dust the dozen or so yards to the phone, blew surplus sand and dirt off the earpiece and scraped the spiders out of the mouthpiece with a stick. These telephones were dotted about the forward area for emergencies. They were joined to the main camp by a thin black-coated wire. If a bulldozer hadn't mangled it or if the wild dogs hadn't chewed through it on its way through the bush to the switchboard, this line kept you in reasonable contact.

Winding a handle and squeezing a lever I listened until a sleepy voice inquired 'Yeah?'

It was certainly hot in the sun so, just as sleepily, I asked if I could talk to the people at my H.Q. in Adelaide. It was much later—I knew how long by the number of flies that had found me clutching the telephone—that I was replying to a voice from Adelaide six hundred miles away. I said: 'Oh! It's only Len here and I was thinking of going to England.'

The arrangements had started. That was late in April 1959. Now here I was in June asking another sort of operator in San Francisco how to work a television set.

THERE had been times when I had almost given up the idea of overseas travel, what with the passport, inoculations, international vaccination certificates, taxation clearance, visitor's visas, spare passport photographs, traveller's cheques, itinerary and books of airline tickets. The number of things required seemed endless, I thought, after I'd ambled into the airline office in Adelaide. I'd told them of my idea about going for a bit of a trip around the world as I thought that would be a better plan than going direct to England. After a closer inspection of the cardboard globe of the world in the mess at Woomera, it seemed a good thing to go over the USA and come home around the other side of the cardboard. The man in the Adelaide office was very pleasant and immediately set about doing his very best for me, suggesting, adding or deleting to a flight plan as we talked, the result being quite an interesting route to the UK. The return trip was in the form of an open ticket leaving the details to be added in London when I was ready. He had concluded with the observation that it was certainly easy to deal with a bushman for such a comprehensive sort of trip, mentioning that he had read about some of my desert expeditions in the newspaper.

There was to be an amazing coincidence involving this man half way through this trip, which I could not possibly have known then, sitting in this Adelaide airline office.

I had been used to carrying a spare shirt with me in the bush for special use on the occasional return to civilisation and so far this seemed all the luggage I'd be taking with me. I couldn't imagine what people carried in all the usual bags, trunks and suitcases they dragged about with them. But I conceded to bring an old leather horse-and-buggy Gladstone bag for the desert boots and a belt with watch and penknife pouches attached. I wanted to take a photograph of Stonehenge so I added a camera.

It was at Honolulu that the lady in a skirt resembling a spinifex bush placed a large ring of flowers around my neck as I plodded down the steps off the plane, making me feel like a ploughing horse in a floral collar. I wondered what I was supposed to do with it and I was glad at the same time that none of my aboriginal friends in Australia could have seen me then. I could actually hear them in between fits of hysteria saying 'That one, he look like a properly pretty fella alright.'

Just before entering the airport building still wearing my mobile flower bed, a huge fellow in uniform stopped me and asked: 'Say, you wanna Cadillac limousine to take you to your hotel?' This sounded a bit rich for me so I thanked him anyway and went on into the customs. A most distracting looking girl in a snappy uniform and cap confronted me and asked me for my name, but when I discovered that I couldn't speak, I handed her my passport. She was a Chinese American with a flashing smile constructed with a combination of dazzling white even teeth and full red lips, I noticed, as she ran an olive smooth finger down a list in an enormous black book on her desk.

'Beadell, now let's see...'

Soon she snapped shut the great thick book and with an extra-stunning smile handed me back my passport and purred '*Waal,* now it looks like you must'a been a good boy 'cause you ain't in our book, so welcome to the USA.'

I found I had to close up my mouth which had been sagging open in order to thank her and ask her what the big black book was all about. She replied in her silky voice 'Why honey you just take a look for your own self,' as she turned the volume around for me to see. It was an alphabetical list of wanted international criminals and known dope pushers.

She continued to examine the book for the next person in the line, as I picked myself up from the ground where I'd fallen after stumbling over someone's bag behind me. I'm sure I detected a desperate and furtive look on the face of the person at present under scrutiny. Although it was a woman of at least eighty-five, heaven knows how much heroin she had secreted away in her hearing-aid batteries.

Once through the customs where the officers microscopically examined my penknife pouch for signs of smuggling on the grounds that it just couldn't be 'for real', I asked another girl at a counter if I could leave my Gladstone bag at the airport. I was due to carry on in a few days and it would save making my side brown as I carried it about; it was still sprinkled with genuine Australian dust from the bush. She pointed to a bank of safe boxes with their keys already inserted where I could leave it for a dime, meaning I had to change my first traveller's cheque for US money. She was pleased to help me and was equally as jolly as the girl with the black book, even though she was disappointed that I didn't carry my plastic boomerang with me when she found I had just arrived from Australia. She explained which of the coins was the dime I'd need to open the safe box, which would release the key once it was opened. The door duly opened and after rolling up my spare shirt, I inserted the bag, clicked shut the door and extracted the key. Just as the door slammed home I noticed—too late—a list of instructions on the inside of it, so opened it again to read them. Being in possession of the facts I again shut the door but the key wouldn't come out or worse still it refused to open either so I asked the girl what had gone wrong. She explained that the one dime operated it once only and changed two nickels into another dime for me. As I began to walk away at last with the key an attendant inquired how long would I be leaving my bag there, advising me that after a day he would be coming around and if he didn't find a further coin inside with my bag, then he would take out the lock altogether with his master key leaving me to pay the difference when I returned. After again opening the door to leave a quarter inside and in the confusion, I clicked shut the door. Of course I'd done it again so returned to the counter for the third time to obtain change in dimes once more. By this time the girl just broke into peals of laughter informing me that my money sure wouldn't last long at this rate.

I couldn't help agreeing with her and I found a cab to take me to the hotel. The driver told me that it would cost me plenty. He went on to say, as we drove, that if I had taken the normal way, the fare is shared by about eight people. Already suspecting his answer I nevertheless asked him just what was the normal way and I was right first off 'Why, in a Cadillac limousine of course.'

The hotel room didn't provide a list of instructions to go with it as much as I found one was needed. There were knobs and buttons coming from all directions, for cool air, warm air, fresh air, light switches and radio music and a few I couldn't work out. The shower room had a different sized towel for each function, but I didn't discover that until I'd dried my tooth brush in one seven feet long, leaving one of eighteen inches square to use after my shower. The basin was equipped with a battery of taps for water ranging from boiling to almost solid ice and I became wary of those after melting the end off a block of soap and turning purple as I froze under another. I never did discover what another flat china affair was for except that it was ideal for scrubbing feet in.

It was a good thing the weather was so hot I thought, as I searched in vain for a bed. The door was about a foot thick and, thinking a bed might be in there, I opened a false compartment only to find it empty. It seemed incredible with all the other things in the room that there was no bed to sleep in. However, I could get some warmth with the floor mat over me if it should turn cold in the night and use a pile of towels for a pillow. Later on I saw a pillow through a crack in a panel along one wall. If I could get it out, it would save using the wet towels. I edged it along to where I could touch it, thankful that I had thought to strap on my knife and pouch at the airport. Soon I had hold of a small piece. With the effort of tugging it through the crack the pillow burst and out poured a cascade of feathers which buried me lying on the floor. This was how the room service girl found me when she came into the room using her master key. The whites of her eyes showed in sharp contrast to her ebony skin as she stared at the scene. I understood how odd I must have appeared at first glance as I sat up with the feathers falling from me like a moulting white leghorn chook, but she didn't have to laugh until she collapsed. She recovered enough to call out to her friend passing 'Wadd'ya know Ella, here's a guy who doesn't know we got a diner here and plucks his own chickens.' Soon they were both in tears hugging each other.

I blew a feather out of my mouth and explained that I'd come from Australia and was only trying to get the pillow out through the crack to use with the floor mat for sleeping. This set them off again until they asked what I wanted with a bed so early as the sun hadn't even gone down yet. I pointed out that it wouldn't stay up forever and was getting things ready for when the time did come. She must have known that I wasn't even a distant relative but she looked at the roof without moving her head and said 'Brother!' She explained that she would fix it all up for me as she picked her way through my impromptu snow storm. She daintily touched one of those unlabelled buttons and out shot a full-sized bed from the wall made up with sheets and blankets, but no pillow.

All this would not take me for a look around Honolulu. So wearing desert boots and belt of pouches I eased past the newly-arrived Cadillac limousines trying hard not to look at them and started hiking.

'Wanna buy an automobile?'

It came from a used car dealer in the first hundred yards, with an accent straight out of a movie. After studying his paddock of glittering so-called old cars, I advised him he would be the first on my list as soon as I needed a one.

WAIKIKI beach was outlined by stalls selling shells and one café had an overhanging verandah full of holes. A line of palm trees growing along the sidewalk passed exactly through them before branching out into foliage twice as high as the roof. Each trunk was ringed with pink concrete and as the breeze swayed them about I noticed they never once touched the sides, causing me to think that perhaps the trees had been there first. I was standing on a corner in the shade of another building labelled 'Drugs,' and idly wondered if the owner's name was in the big black book. At first glance I thought it was a chemist's shop.

On the way back to the hotel for some dinner I found it took quite a while to walk past a car parked the wrong way round. It seemed to be rather an ordinary car that had been put on 'the rack' making it twice as long. As I crossed the street, thinking how few cars you see which have had that treatment, I was all but run down by a station wagon at my back. The driver swerved violently with his words lost in the blaring of his horn. I knew I had solved the riddle of the wrong-way parked sausage car and hoped I would live long enough to get the hang of these left-hand drive streets.

Sitting in the dining room I idly watched a well-dressed man finishing his meal. Suddenly he looked furtively about him, slipped something under his plate and hurried away. In seconds a waitress appeared at his table, raised the plate and dropped the object into her apron pocket. Thoroughly curious now and with the black book in mind, I wondered if this was how the pushers operated. It did seem a little less obvious than how I had thought at first: an operator driving a bulldozer with a blade-full of heroin. The whole story was revealed to me by one honest-looking waitress who I had confided in. It turned out to be my first brush with tipping and the amount to leave could easily be worked out provided you had a slide rule on you.

I had flown here from Fiji sitting next to a couple on their way home to New Jersey, who had also stopped off in Hawaii. They were Andy Axtel and his wife who had walked off the plane wearing the most colourful nightgowns possible, which proved they were no strangers to Honolulu. Several days later, not even having visited Pearl Harbor, Andy and his wife were again sitting across the aisle and they were going to fly from San Francisco to New York. Andy was to eventually help me through the maze in New York a month later, but now as we waited for take off I told them of my experiences since last seeing them, discovering that the huge building covered with ledges was actually a hotel, and not all hotels had their pillows so hard to get at.

Soon the engineer of the aircraft came to me, confirmed my name and explained that his sister worked for the Woomera project; he asked how long I planned to stop over in *Frisco*.

Later, when discussing our plans, I casually used the word *Frisco* when chatting to Andy. There followed an uneasy silence. It seemed 'S.F.' could be tolerated, so could San Francisco, but never *Frisco*, at least by anyone living there. I had so much to learn.

The Golden Gate Bridge showed through the clouds by the time I had got through explaining to an elderly couple why we were landing here yesterday when it should have been tomorrow. I had drawn the diagrams of the earth and sun, the Greenwich meridian and the International Date Line near New Zealand on the back of a white paper bag which I now threw into the trash and studied the coastline around S.F.

At the airport terminal I had lost Andy in the fuss of retrieving the Gladstone bag which I had successfully extracted from the safe box in Honolulu, minus the quarter, only to see him later waiting for his wife on a chair in the building. I was recovering from my experience of nearly falling on my face as I went to open the door of the terminal. It had flown open by itself as I approached and reached out for it, but I consoled myself that at least I knew all about safe boxes by then. Andy asked me where I would be staying and, as I answered, a blank look came to his face. I vaguely remembered the place had something to do with old-time mariners and was really called The Drake Wiltshire and not Vasco da Gama as I had told him. His wife arrived and they invited me to ride into town with them in their cab. I couldn't think of a good reason not to, and we walked out with the Cadillac limousine episode still fresh in my mind.

Andy was all for the idea I had thought out of hiring a car and driving across the USA. The trip to the Drake Wiltshire altered my ideas about that, however, as the cars were all travelling at seventy miles per hour bumper to bumper and the cabbies were carrying on conversations with friends in vehicles alongside. I had been used to travelling at seventy miles a week with mulga trees alongside and wanted to survive long enough to get back to them if possible. Leaning over, Andy gave me a card with his address on it three thousand miles away and asked me to call them when I got to New York and they would show me around. I gladly agreed to do so in about a month's time and ventured into the lobby of my new hotel clutching my spare shirt.

Sure enough, my name was right there on the register and a little old man in uniform grabbed my arm and quickly bow-legged his way to the elevator. He must have been eighty. Following him into the lift I realised he was one of these 'bell boys' I had heard of. He gripped my belongings in such a way that I would have to fight him for them if I wanted them back. He opened the door and charged into the room, flinging back curtains, opening windows, spinning knobs on the wall and tearing a coloured rag cover off the bed, and finished up standing in front of me panting with the effort. The only way I could pry my shirt out of his hand was by buying it back from him with a quarter. I noticed when he slammed shut the door that it had a wide gap between it and the floor. The reason for this became obvious the next morning when four newspapers were forced into the room. They were two inches thick. The door itself was a foot thick and I found that anything you put in the cupboard—after I discovered what it was—disappeared by the time you next went to get it. Luckily I had only lost my shirt in it, but when I checked later there it was once again. It seemed that anything you put in it was taken away by the laundry people using an outside panel opening. I made sure I didn't put my desert boots in it.

That was when I noticed the glass-fronted T.V. box and rang the operator about it. We had quite a conversation about kangaroos and boomerangs before she purred that she was sorry she didn't have the time right then to come up herself and personally show me how it worked. I found these operators very friendly, calling you honey without even seeing you. At least she knew by then that I really wasn't kidding. I had been frightened of breaking something off as it didn't look very strong, but following her instructions it came on at last, whereupon I thanked her and she finished off with 'You're welcome.' I wondered if that meant to San Francisco or the Drake Wiltshire, but whatever it meant it sounded very bright and cheerful, as I settled down to watch the picture of a wire-haired terrier selling bulldozers.

The clerk at the desk in the lobby informed me there were tickets available to see some of the sights by coach. Soon I was off to see Alcatraz jail on the Dock, to travel over the Golden Gate Bridge to the Muir redwood forests and to visit other places. I set off for a hike before the first trip was due. Passing a corner where a crane was systematically bashing down a building with a huge iron ball, I saw a complete tram come down a steep hill only to disappear clean out sight. Thinking *that* was something you don't see every day, I went to investigate. The illusion was caused by the tram momentarily disappearing from view as it dipped into the terrace of the cross street. Following the tram down the hill I discovered that the concrete was as rough as any mountain range. It was specially made with a trowel to prevent anybody wearing hob-nailed boots from falling over and slipping down the one in four grade. The parked cars were all angled into the gutter so they couldn't roll forwards if the holding gear failed. This way they could only tumble over sideways. Ambling around San Francisco was like taking a stroll over the Swiss Alps. The first bus driver to take one of my tickets told us sleepily that this was really a quiet and peaceful place where nothing much ever happened apart from an occasional earthquake and fire which would demolish everything. He described their underground car park hewn from solid rock and lined with reinforced concrete. It could hold thousands of cars giving visitors an idea of just how many relations the City Fathers had. You never knew when an atomic attack could happen nowadays.

The next point of interest was the only hotel in San Francisco with a bar in every room. It turned out to be Alcatraz.

At another stop we were required to observe an enormous plumbob swinging slowly on a long piano wire showing the revolutions of the earth on a large graduated circle. On a visit to the Golden Gate Bridge a cross-section of the cable holding up the bridge was to be seen at one end of the structure, and it was really slightly larger than I had imagined from photographs. I had thought that it would need to be quite strong, however, this multi-cored section was beyond a joke, as was the price per foot which would have gone a long way to reducing our national debt.

Everyone had told the engineer who had designed and built the bridge that it would fall over as soon as it was finished, but he went ahead anyway. It stood up to our weight quite well as we drove across it to continue on to the redwoods.

The trees in the Muir Forest are the oldest in the world being three hundred feet high and a thousand years of age. They would be even more now as that was in 1959. They were certainly a change from our mulga scrub in Central Australia.

Back at the hotel room after that trip I found there was time to ring a number which had been given to me by a friend in Australia. I picked up the spiderless telephone and called the operator once more. Feeling a little relieved as it sounded like a different one this time, I read out my number from where I'd written it, on the back of a bully beef tin label, and waited. This operator soon proved equally as cheerful as the first as she replied with 'Sure honey.' In a little while her pleasant voice again came to me over the wire: 'Gee! I'm sorry sugar, but your sweetie's not answering.' I hastened to explain, whereupon she breezily continued on with 'but well now, let's see how I'm fixed.'

Nothing seemed too much trouble for these friendly telephone girls who never failed to end every call with a bright 'You're welcome.' I began wondering whether I would survive the rest of the trip across the USA. The conversation somehow drifted to the outback country in Australia and how the government pay people about four dollars for the scalp of a wild dog. She whistled into the phone and asked 'Saay! if they hand you four bucks for a scalp, then how much would you get for the whole thing?'

I was booked on an aeroplane to Los Angeles for the following afternoon. After the gentle seventy mile-an-hour drive back to the airport I retrieved the Gladstone bag and replaced my shirt. Soon S.F. was lost to view beneath the fog which regularly envelops Alcatraz and I found I was curious to discover what the telephone operators were like in Los Angeles.

Chapter 2

IT'S QUITE O.K. TO SAY L.A.

THE room to which the seventy-five year-old bell 'boy' took me in the Statler Hotel contained a television set as well. I was an expert by this time, so I switched it on after the bell boy had gone. The fact that he had departed with a tip proved that he had outwitted me on this occasion. American hotel staff will hang around indefinitely for a tip, until it becomes impossible to pretend they're not there.

We had circled over Los Angeles before landing. I saw how the roads were heaped up on top of each other, with the traffic going at a great rate in every direction. The tremendous proportions of the city really struck me. The cab ride from the airport confirmed my decision not to use a hire car to drive over to New York, but fly as planned.

The lobby was full of *real* plants growing out of *real* earth, with green glazed tiles paving the concrete. The effect was very pleasant and cool looking, with the front doors opening out on to a covered way where taxis and coaches could unload or collect passengers and their bags. The old horse-and-buggy Gladstone was once again in a safe box at the airport and I was wondering just why I had brought it along in the first place. My shirt, at present hanging on its own in the large wardrobe, could have easily fitted into a saddlebag along with the desert boots.

Los Angeles was flat and sprawling compared to the hilly compact S.F. Walking around for the rest of the day, with tickets for the next day's coach trips, justified the impression from the air. On one concrete sidewalk I saw a two-foot cube with no lid. There was nothing unusual about that, but it was the head and shoulders of the man in it which caught my eye. They were just showing above the rim of the box and his arms moved about with a can for donations in one hand, leaving the other free to touch his hat as the coins chinked into it. As the sides of the box were only two feet long and the rim fitted tightly under his armpits, I concluded the rest of him must have been standing in a manhole. This all seemed to be a good attention grabber. I watched fascinated, as a car pulled up alongside and two men came over from it, picked up the box with its contents by the handles and bundled it and its occupant into the trunk. As they drove to greener pastures I was horrified to see there was no hole, just concrete where the box had been standing.

Every few steps someone would stop me and beg a dime for a cup of coffee. Most of them could hardly stand upright, their eyes would try and focus on something two feet above my head, and I wondered what sort of coffee they drank here. Maybe they just thought I was very tall, but it saved me many dimes.

Why they ever called an area as flat as the Nullarbor Plain *downtown L.A.* I couldn't figure out. Nevertheless, I was soon in *downtown Los Angeles*, attracted to a large store window along with a hundred other people.

As I edged through the crowd the reason for it all immediately became apparent. There was a dummy, dressed in a tuxedo, with an electric wire running from it. It was standing upright as it turned to the left, and bowed then turned to the right, and bowed and so on, without stopping and with electronic precision. I was puzzled by the curiosity caused by such a model, while I mentally figured out what it must have looked like inside. It must have had a motor similar to that of a car windshield wiper. It was the fixed staring eyes in a waxen face which tended to spoil the effect. Surely these could have been brought to life by some sort of electric solenoid. It was then I began to listen to the conversations around me. 'See, it moved further that time.'

'No, I done lined up its nose with the model of the rattlesnake behind it, and it moved the same both times.'

'Then you must'a moved.' Another couple were arguing: 'Look at that sweat under its eyes.'

'That's water oozing through the papier-mâché under the wax.' The discussions went on as did the dummy, and I found myself looking more closely. After another half an hour I couldn't detect anything of the action of a windshield wiper. As I was about to give up and continue hiking, the 'Thing' smiled, blinked its eyes, waved cheerily to the crowd and walked back out of the window with a short length of flex trailing behind. Everyone gasped at the amazing feat of controlled co-ordination of muscles. I thought he would be good at stalking game in the bush.

I WAS still trudging about the outskirts of the city after nightfall, when something happened to make me think that this was about as far as I was going to get on my trip. It was in a particularly dingy sort of region, with darkened figures lurking in doorways, in unlit narrow alleys. I could hear the sirens of police patrol cars shrieking in the distance, on their way to some new crisis. It never seemed to let up through the night. There was a constant screech of tyres as they took corners on two wheels. It added considerably to the atmosphere. I started wishing I had left the wallet I had made out of the canvas of an old tent flap back in my room at the Statler.

I had just crossed over the lead off into one of these blackened alleys when it happened. As I put one desert boot onto the sidewalk, after stepping over the pile of trash in the gutter, a body reeled out of the darkness to fall at my feet in the semi-gloom. A little light was cast by the hooded lights of an 'adult only' movie den on the opposite side. The body belonged to a man dressed in a torn black suit. He had tousled oily black hair above an ashen face streaked with blood. He lay on his back on the toe of my desert boot. I thought that *here* was something you didn't see every night. At that instant a police siren behind me grew louder. The white doors on the otherwise black car blurred into view, and stopped in a squeal of protesting rubber beside us. The flashing light continued to operate, as the wail of the siren died. Two uniformed officers spilled out to charge towards us. The brass cartridges in their heavy gun belts glinted momentarily. The butts of their revolvers also shone, as they sagged at their sides. I stood open-mouthed, staring at them over the inert body. I pointed down at the body and told them that somebody seemed to be lying on my foot. It must have sounded as though I was in the habit of finding blood-soaked bodies lying about. I thought it was useless to tell them I didn't do it, and began to have visions of the D.A. in L.A. issuing an indictment, or whatever. It was at the thirteenth precinct too. I was about to tell them 'I ain't going to say nuttin' until I call a mouthpiece,' but instead they brushed me aside without even looking at me. They seized the body, which was by now feeling like a dead weight on my foot, and dragged it into their car. Slamming the doors, they were off all in the one action, with their siren wailing. Those tormented tyres were still trying to explain to anyone interested that they would be happy to retire from the police force anytime.

Releasing my breath in a long low wheeze, I stood there in the pools of drying blood and assumed the coincidence of timing must have come in the form of an anonymous phone call. They were probably told that if they went to that corner they would find a stiff. I just happened to be standing under the victim at the time.

Back in the hotel room, to which I retreated before I pushed my luck any further, I switched on the television set. It seemed I was safe at last, that is until it warmed up to show the programme under way: *Dragnet*. It sure was true to life—or death—depending upon how you looked at it.

Next morning the bus for the ticket holders to Disneyland and Knott's Berry Farm pulled into the covered way at the front doors. As other tourists had been collected on the way, I asked a small girl if she'd mind me sitting in the vacant seat next to her. She smiled and said 'Sure—you're welcome.' By the time we had reached the stacked-up roads, I had learnt that her name was Sherry and she was on holiday from Hawaii. Her mother and little brother were sitting behind us. We arrived at Disneyland after battling our way through the oil well derricks next to the eight-lane freeway. I had obtained a much clearer picture of Hawaii, while she gained many facts about kangaroos in Central Australia.

As we walked to the entrance gates, with the bed of flowers growing on a grass ramp depicting Mickey Mouse, Sherry's mother pleaded with me to look after her children. We were to meet her back at the bus when it was time to leave. They had apparently worn her out already. As I was only too pleased, we left her to take her rest and went inside.

I wondered how they iced the scale model of the Matterhorn which reared-up dominating everything. Finally I decided quick-setting white plastic must have been poured from helicopters. The look of the bathrooms of the future was a feature in an area called Tomorrowland. They seemed as if they could cope with every function called for, in an average-sized castle. They had everything except a waterproof videophone. There were marching girls to help you feel glad you weren't at the real Matterhorn, mainly because of the intense cold they would feel in their present attire. Full-sized jazz bands were being conducted by any small child who came forward. Sherry conducted their playing of *When the Saints Go Marching In* and it didn't sound any different to when the regular leader had the baton.

Profile cut-out artists and demonstrators of card tricks lined the mock-up thoroughfare called Main Street USA. For a nickel you could have a newspaper printed with your own name in headlines across the front page, telling readers all about your visit to Disneyland. The Indian camp had a very authentic feel to it, with teepees made of old worn animal hides, with Indians sitting around camp fires. I stopped myself just in time from squatting down with them, as I had done with desert aborigines in Australia.

Sherry and her brother, having a better knowledge of Disneyland than me, from television and movies, were guiding me about. Eventually they thought they'd like to return to the bus to fetch a camera from their 'Mom'. At the exit gates a man, without even looking up, grabbed my hand and brought his fist down on my wrist. I was about to fight back when the children assured me it was O.K. and we passed out for the camera. Returning to the entrance, another man grasped my hand and nearly dragged me off my feet. He pulled my hand towards him and held it under a vertical tube. I was amazed to see a green phosphorescent spot suddenly appear on my wrist. He opened the gate for me to re-enter, after thoughtfully giving me back my hand, and I spilled inside. Examining my hand again I couldn't see a thing: the spot had disappeared from sight. It was all carefully explained by Sherry. She told me how the ultra-violet rays had actuated the radioactive spot placed there by the first hand-grabber. Testing the spot several months later, at the atomic research establishment with a similar torch, I was relieved to see it had gone away. It only lasts until the first bath after the ordeal.

I was specially interested in the artists who would draw a crayon portrait of anyone for a dollar. Sherry took her brother off to inspect Fantasyland for a while, as I watched them. Cute little pony-tailed girls in sailor's suits, small boys, men and women were depicted perfectly in the allotted time. It took only seven minutes to produce these cartoons on the sheets of paper which subjects had bought for a dollar. Just as I was about to volunteer—not as a subject but as an artist—to draw one of them working there, a well-dressed man in a brown suit and hat came to stand beside me. He inquired in his very pleasant way if I was enjoying my visit here. I replied that it was really 'beaut,' whereupon he informed me that I had come from Australia. I wondered how he knew. He went on to say he was somewhat of a stranger here himself, having come down from Canada in his capacity as a film distributor, to negotiate dealings at Hollywood. In three minutes he knew my name as well as my room number in the Statler. He seemed such a nice man. He bought me a glass of lemonade and asked me if I would care to accompany him on his mission to Hollywood the following day. Although I already had a bus ticket for Hollywood I agreed eagerly. With that he walked off, interested in everything around him, saying he would ring me up in the morning.

Sherry came back as the bus was soon due to go. We left this amazing place of variety—from the castle of Sleeping Beauty to Indian tepees—to the mercies of the visitors. I hoped to return one day. We were soon on the way to Knott's Berry Farm, radioactive stamp on our hands and all.

IT seems that a long time ago a Mr and Mrs Knott had a berry farm. They also served meals to weary travellers on their way to L.A. These meals of blueberry or chicken pie became well-known. They had to expand their output to the stage where they required twenty-two chicken ranches to supply enough birds for each day's meals, which by then numbered five thousand. As the freeways developed, their project flourished and the not-so weary travellers continued to arrive. The Knotts provided entertainment for visitors by having a complete wild western town moved, stick by stick, and re-erected on their farm. It was recreated exactly as the frontier town it had been many miles away. There was a livery stable, a saloon with bat-wing doors and a blacksmith's shop housing a weather-beaten old smith. He was making shoes for the stage horses. There was even a Sheriff's office. It was just as it had been, faded signs, boardwalks, stray bullet holes and all. There was a small section of a narrow-gauge rail link from the Denver and Rio Grande line, called the Calico Railroad. There was a hangman's tree and, to complete the scene, an adobe chapel.

The old lady who got off the coach in front of us suddenly let out a squeal, throwing her arms up in the air. We looked past her to see the cause of her concern. A grizzled old cow-hand had her covered with a Colt six-gun. He stood on his bow legs, covered with buckskin chaps. He was eyeing her belligerently, with blue eyes set in his leathery old face. His features were partly hidden by bristling white stubble under a battered Stetson, turned up at the front. He was leading a fully-laden burro carrying camping gear, a gold prospecting dish and a shovel with a worn rawhide halter. He croaked an order to the frail old lady to 'Git movin', the words sliding unobstructed over his toothless gums.   A dozen or so photographs were taken of the gun slinger. A stagecoach drew in periodically, taking people for rides through the badlands. Sherry and her brother climbed up. A dusty old shotgun guard sat on top next to the driver, with a solid-looking iron box under his knees. As soon as the coach was full of delighted children he unwound the lines from the brake lever and they were off through the sage brush. After a time the galloping horses careered back to stop in a cloud of dust. Sherry came racing over to tell the news of the hold-up of the stagecoach. It had been robbed of the iron box by several masked desperadoes.   They had shot the driver, the evidence of which was to be seen; his hastily tied bandanna was used as a sling. The shotgun guard had had time to get one of them before collecting a slug in his leg.

At the gold mine there was a creek which a ragged old prospector had staked out for himself. He would let children in if they had a *ticket* in the form of a small glass bottle, which they would buy for ten cents, to try their luck. The bottle was to hold the colour of gold which would invariably be found in each dish of dirt they panned, the old timer showing them how. Soon Sherry and her brother came back excitedly waving their strike.   The Knotts must have been wonderful people.

The trip back to L.A. was packed with talk about the day's events, which would have been a highlight in the life of children and adults alike. I very reluctantly farewelled Sherry and her family as we drew up under the covered way at the Statler.

MY ticket to Hollywood was for the following afternoon, but early in the morning the bedside phone rang. It was Mason as arranged. He told me he would meet me in the lobby at ten. Exactly on time Mason stepped into the lobby, not from the main entrance where I had been looking, but through a rear door. He explained there was less traffic out that way. He mentioned that his car was parked down the block and we walked off through the back door.

Outside a very short round man bumped into Mason. He was approaching from the other direction and apologised for his clumsiness. Mason said to him that his accent meant he wasn't from L.A. The round man agreed with him, explaining that he'd 'Done just got in from Kentucky,' as his mother-in-law had died. Mason filled in the rest of the sad details for him observing '…and you came up to bury her.' This all sounded a little odd for someone who had indicated that he was in such a hurry. I was growing more suspicious by the minute.

'I came to bury my mother-in-law.'

Mason merely continued with how he'd come from Canada, and that I had come from Australia. Within a minute they were ignoring me, as they flipped a coin into the air and guessed at the results. All this was in the middle of the footpath. On the first try Mason lost and gave the round man a dollar bill, confirming that they played this game in Kentucky as well as Canada. They both suddenly remembered me and asked if we played it in Australia. I was invited to have a go. We were supposed to be on our way to

Hollywood, but I gravely doubted it would be Mason with whom I'd be going. I checked my belt watch for the departure time of the coach. I regarded their proffered nickel as one would a rattlesnake, refusing to lay a finger on it. The round one walked over to a shop window behind Mason. Leaning on it, he began tying his shoelace. As Mason saw me looking over his shoulder— at who I was sure by now was his partner—he passed the incident off, by saying not to mind him as he was only fixing his shoe. That remark settled it: they were con men. The round man could have been standing on his head for all Mason could see, yet here he was describing to me just what he was doing. Their whole complicated scheme was now clear to me, so I decided to have some fun with them instead. When Mason was joined by his colleague, they again handed me a nickel, which I took this time and pushed it down into my desert boot, much to their open-mouthed astonishment. I explained that I never gambled, but was willing to carry on with the game if I could use the doubled-headed coin in my boot. They both dissolved into the crowd with Mr Five's short legs working like piston rods past a huge uniformed cop wearing a gun belt. I was glad they hadn't thought of stopping to tell him that there was a 'guy wearing a hunting knife on his belt back a bit with a double-headed nickel in his desert boot.' I made my way back to the hotel laughing at the picture of a spherical human rolling down the slope past the cop trying to keep up with Mason. The whole operation had already cost them my bottle of lemonade.

The bus for Hollywood pulled up under the covered way by the front door of the Statler. After dinner of blueberry pie— probably courtesy of the Knotts—it was not long before we were driving along Hollywood Boulevard. The first impression was that, without the invention of glass, there would have been nothing there at all. I imagined it would have closely resembled a bush fire if seen at night.

There was one place that no one seemed to be able to leave alone whilst it was being built. People would scratch their names into the cement before it had time to dry at the entrance to the building which went by the name of *Grauman's Chinese Theater.* It had become so bad, that the owners had not even bothered to fill in all the squares, knowing what would happen. Everywhere else had smooth, unmolested cement outside the door. It was near a corner and I wondered why the Asian gentlemen had not been to the police, until I read some of the names of the vandals. I'm sure I had heard of some them somewhere. There was 'Hopalong Cassidy,' who had added the impression of two revolvers to his name. A lady had pressed a pair of ice skates into the wet cement, with the name Sonja Henie inscribed between them. Perhaps it wasn't the work of vandals after all, I thought, as I saw a fellow who called himself Will Rogers with horse tracks around his mark. Most of them could have been done without anyone seeing, but you could hardly miss a horse mooching about on the sidewalk. By the time I had read through them all I was certain I'd heard of them before in an occasional movie I had seen on brief visits to civilisation. I thought of one man I'd seen once, called Jimmy Durante. I wondered what he would have pushed into cement next to his name.

It wasn't far to Beverly Hills from Hollywood. I couldn't help noticing that Sunset Boulevard was somehow different to my Gunbarrel Highway we'd made across Central Australia only the year before. Green expanses of lawn had taken the place of the spinifex plains I'd been used to. Instead of mulga trees there were magnolias and shaved hedges. The lawns had the appearance of having been vacuum cleaned every morning. Another difference was the addition of houses and, compared to my road where there was not a single dwelling of any kind for nine hundred miles, these places at least looked strong enough to stand up to the dust storms which would reduce our canvas awnings to shreds in seconds. The bus driver informed us that a Miss Jayne Mansfield lived in one of the places. There was something about that name which sounded familiar, I thought, as we passed another rather nice-looking place which Dinah Shore called home. I knew of her that she was good at singing. Randolf Scott kept the rain off in another impressive homestead, and I also knew that he had done a bit of bushwork in his time. I would have liked to have had a yarn with him. Charles Boyer's home was rather hard to see through all the foliage. The coach driver assured us that Charles didn't camp in a tent behind it all.

I missed seeing an address I'd heard of somewhere, a number 77 Sunset Strip, but there was another address I did see which I had also heard of, later in the year: a number 10 Downing Street.

As we drove away from this jungle of swimming pools and orchid scrub, I reflected I had always thought there must be an easier way to earn a living. I had thought this in my normal surroundings in Australia, with the flies and the nearest water five hundred miles away. The quantity of water in any one of the private swimming pools here would have been enough to easily last me for a year.

We soon came to a beach called Santa Monica, with the Pacific Ocean lapping onto the sand. We were instructed that, if we wanted to see a real live film star, then 'all eyes left.' Here was a large establishment made of windows held together with strips of rock, facing west. A thin man sat looking out towards the horizon: so this was the famous Stan Laurel of the *Laurel and Hardy* films of the thirties. He had brought laughter to so many people for many years, including myself a quarter of a century before. He had lost his more substantial mate and it was kind of sad to realise that he would never again feature in a slapstick movie or children's comic book again.

Back in L.A., and in the middle of a paddock, a jazz session seemed to be under way. This was the closing of the Hollywood Exhibition, so I headed to the area. I was using my last night to further explore this great city—keeping away from the thirteenth precinct. As I leaned against a *trash barrel*, I noticed the meeting was attended solely by Negroes who were in fact holding a church service. Their hymn singing sounded much more lovely than I'd ever heard before. The minister in charge of the gathering spoke with passion, the beads of perspiration glistening on his face, above shouted approvals from his congregation.

Keeping on the move for fear of meeting up with another Mason, I walked along one of the brightest streets. Picture theatres were showing movies starring people whose houses and names in cement I had seen only that afternoon. Knowing that my spiderless telephone would be ringing at my ear early the following morning, I made my way back to the Statler. The phone would be reminding me that my airline's transport would be calling for me at the hotel for the onward flight.

I went to sleep wondering about the answer to the question that had been nagging me since the day before. Why did they ever call the track out of Los Angeles which had cost them $158,000,000 a 'freeway?'

The jangling of the phone penetrated my head in the morning. A girl's brisk voice told me the time for pick up. I said, in a sleepy voice, that she was very kind and thanked her from the bottom of my leaden eyelids. I heard the friendly 'You're welcome' just before dropping the receiver on the floor, missing the hook by a foot.

As the long, gleaming car lumbered to the airport at eighty miles an hour, I thought of the beaten-up man in the tuxedo and how he had taken a different sort of airborne trip, without the need for the aeroplane.

Chapter 3

THE CAMP IN THE CACTUS

'PASSENGERS on flight U.A. 714—LA to Las Vegas: your aircraft is now ready through gate number five, all aboard please.' My horse-and-cart Gladstone bag had already been electronically rolled away through a flap behind the desk at the airport building in LA and I had been sitting down waiting for this message to emerge. Flights had already left for 'Ceeaddle' and San Diego as I idly watched other passengers feverishly working the slot machines to get their supply of tranquilliser pills labelled 'freedom from household drudgery pills,' 'air-sickness pills', pills for depression and pills for over-elation, 'happy pills' and 'miserable pills.' I thought the spherical man from Kentucky had taken some of the latter as the best remedy for his mother-in-law. Some came up with hot or cold coffee, hamburgers and soda to take with all the pills. I received enough therapy by just watching. Studying the Systems Map I endeavoured to locate this 'Ceeaddle' and came to the conclusion that it must have been a town shown a long way to the north spoken in American. I was able to confirm this later in Arizona where I discovered that the ranches there raised 'caddle.'

As the pilot ran-up the engines at the end of the strip, a most cheerful hostess with a dazzling smile leant over to me and asked 'Honey, why don't I sit in this vacant seat next to you for the take off?' Try as I did, I couldn't think of any reason whatever why she should not, so I tried out my new language which I'd learned from Sherry:

'Sure, be my guest.'

'Thanks a lot baby,' she said to which I replied:

'You're welcome,'

as she sat down in the cutest way and buckled the seat-belt. I thought I was catching on to this pleasant language but wasn't too sure about the 'baby' bit. She could see I was more than six weeks old just as I could see she was herself but she continued on with:

'Boy! I hope you have yourself a ball in Vegas, but...'

she laid her hand on my arm and I almost died on the spot.

'Watch out for your money like a good kid.'

I didn't seem to be able to grow up at all, but I was grateful I had progressed from babyhood past kid and onto boy at least. I thought by the time we landed at Vegas, I'd be drawing the pension at this rate.

I told her not to worry as I didn't gamble, recounting the Mason story and was just beginning to imagine that she took me for a Texan when she went on with the conversation.

'Man, I guess all those kangaroos must be getting real lonely over there without you.' That bush life in Australia must have shown more than I thought but I noted that I had at last graduated from 'boy' into 'man,' and I kept my fingers crossed in case I might get 'Daddy' next time.

She hadn't imagined there were so many aerodynamic problems involved in the construction of boomerangs, or that drought-stricken jack rabbits really did learn to climb mulga trees for food, but by the time we were circling over Las Vegas she was quite an authority on Central Australia.

L AS Vegas from the air had a very similar appearance to Woomera if you exchanged the salt bush and gibber stones surrounding the rocket range town for cactus and sage brush and cut the buttes right off, instead of only just the tops. Amongst the fruit machines at the airport were notice boards listing the live entertainment currently on show. As I went over to one of the fruit machines I realised not only pills came from these things and looked forward to having an apple while waiting for the bus. Several others with the same idea were trying to get something to eat, but their machines didn't seem to be working as they pushed coin after coin into them. There was a hole at the bottom large enough for a watermelon to pass through and I wondered how you selected what you wanted.

I was booked into the Hotel Riviera. Driving to the hotel on a track across the desert known as The Strip I decided that my first impression from the air, of Las Vegas being similar to Woomera, was fast disappearing. I saw a huge glass fish bowl above the ground but as we approached I was surprised to see the swimming 'fish' were wearing bikinis. Nearby an enormous hour-glass seemed to take on a different appearance with the addition of a lady's head and shoulders drawn on top of it at a place which was called The Sands.

As we travelled nobody could help but notice the thirty-foot high statue of a sheik dressed in yellow complete with turban and fish hook shoes on top of a brightly-coloured hotel next to a sign—The Dunes—which you could read perfectly well without binoculars at twenty miles. I had spent a good many years in Australia getting these things flattened for my road, but it would take more than our one bulldozer to move this one. The cactus depicted on *The Desert Inn* was certainly of Texan proportions. At another place there seemed to be a lot of water going to waste cooling a pink tower with dozens of strikingly arranged sprays outside a building called Hotel Tropicana.

Eventually a solid-looking structure materialised out of the heat haze across the desert with slots along the walls and the letter 'R' on top of Central Australian proportions. The word *Riviera* appeared vertically over a porch: this was where I would be staying for the next few days. Wondering what the slots were for I thought of how my bush swag roll carried out the same functions for sleeping as did this establishment, but at the same time the hotel would be better in a dust storm. As we pulled up I discovered that the slots were lines of verandahs outside the rooms and not for coins at all.

I was forced to bring my Gladstone bag here with me as there were no safe boxes where we landed. The surroundings at last matched my desert boots. As I walked into the lobby with the deep carpet closing over my feet, I had the surprise, so far from home, of running into someone I knew. I couldn't place just where I'd seen him so asked the girl at the desk if she knew who he was before actually going over to interview him. Her friendly reply was 'Sure, who doesn't: that's Nat King Cole.'

As soon as I was relieved of my Gladstone bag in my room— lost amongst the TV, radio, glass desk with its ivory telephone, air conditioning knobs, piles of towels and plastic bags for carrying my wet bikini—I checked to see if I could ever find it again. It was five paces south-west of the door. Then I did something which probably hadn't been done since the gold rush days to California: I hiked the three miles into downtown Las Vegas. If what I'd already seen was only just a lead-in, then the place should prove to be worth seeing.

Through the heat haze on the way I saw one of the largest hob-nailed boots ever revolving around on a post. Trudging closer it looked more like a riding boot, but closer again it proved to be a glittering mercury-coloured, high-heeled shoe the size of an average ready-mix cement truck rotating on a vertical spindle. For want of a better name they called this place The Silver Slipper.

The first thing which came into view on the main street of the village was the tallest building in the area with the name *Hotel Fremont* quite legibly printed on a sign obviously strong enough to support its weight. It was covered with windows and slots, and the main street went by the same name.

Nobody could possibly miss the tremendous neon apparition of a prototype horse thief complete with spurs, Stetson sun bonnet and red scarf waving his arms, tirelessly beckoning 'Pardners' inside his Pioneer Club. I thought at first he was the Drango Kid but he really had the handle of Vegas Vic.

Just before arriving at the main cluster of casinos, I walked past a whitewashed cowshed with a sign painted over the front which caused me to beg the cow's pardon. It read *The Hitching Post Wedding Chapel* where you could get married or divorced, as the case may be. Flowers growing by a low picket fence could be chopped off as you went in for wearing in your buttonhole.

There was a *Lucky Strike Club* with its chuck bar and a picture on its packets of matches of an old-timer panning for gold at a creek. The *Golden Gate Casino* had a picture of the bridge in S.F. coincidentally made of solid gold. The *Westerner* was decorated with wagon wheels and skeletons of cattle. Funnily enough it served Italian food.

All a burglar would need to take the two tremendous nuggets of solid gold away from the roof of an impressive-looking corner establishment would be a helicopter fitted with grappling hooks. The nuggets were on top of *The Golden Nugget Gambling Hall* in golden lights of such a size that I had to walk its full length to read it.

One club in Las Vegas had the really novel name of *The Las Vegas Club* boasting the largest sign west of Chicago. By the look of it there must have been some real ones *east* of Chicago. It came down from somewhere out of the sky to end in a blaze of lights at the bottom.

As I passed by the *Nevada Club* a man at the door asked me my name. He was wearing a .45 on a brass studded gunbelt, so I told him as nicely as I could, whereby he jammed something into my hand ordering me to take it inside to a counter. To keep him happy I hurried over to the counter where another man grabbed at whatever I was clutching and in the space of a few seconds handed me a red oblong of plastic on a small chain with the words *Las Vegas 1959* printed in gold above *Nevada Club*. After I'd made my escape I examined it more closely and found my initials inscribed in gold across the back. This *Nevada Club* showed a cowgirl in the act of catching a shower of coins pouring from a poker machine into the nearest thing available—her own riding skirt. It was quite a useful receptacle and would have settled an age-old question had it been a Scotsman wearing a kilt.

On the opposite side of Fremont Street to the *Golden Nugget*, was the *Horseshoe Club* with its invitation to amble over and see a million dollars, all in the one heap. No cents, just the neat thousand grand. It must have been pushed there with a bulldozer. The *Boulder Club* next door had another tall sign and advised customers that it was as solid as the Boulder Dam. The fact that the dam was now known as the Hoover Dam made me feel sorry for the owners who were too poor to have the sign altered, but it made no difference to the solidity of the club.

The most wonderful sign of all, I thought, was the one which came next in line and spelled out the atmosphere of Las Vegas. It was simply called *The Mint*, and really had to be seen to be believed. From a distance it looked like a gigantic pink curved bridge with white edging, one end rearing up into the sky, its name in different coloured lights on the vertical column. At the top of the column sat a dazzlingly white star of equivalent proportions. The whole thing was switched off entirely every few seconds and would re-grow from the lower end progressively until it burst into the star on top. On a closer look the white edging turned into thousands of electric light bulbs all but touching each other and the pink part of the bridge was made of countless horizontal and vertical neon tubes. The wording of *The Mint* broke into the pink tubing of the column and was written with coloured globes. I secured a photograph of it by standing on the corner of the *Golden Nugget* and operating the camera in the instant it was fully illuminated. I was told that it was one of the brightest signs in the world.

UP to now I'd been hesitant to enter any of these places after the *Nevada Club* episode, but the doors opened on their own, so I walked through. Just as I stepped inside, a loud clanging of bells started up and red lights flashed on and off everywhere. I turned to rush out again but found the doors had snapped shut behind me as I wondered what I'd done wrong this time. I glanced at one of the signs which read *jackpot* at each flash, and saw a customer half-buried in an avalanche of coins coming out of the hole in one of the machines that a watermelon could pass through. Apparently the place went berserk when anyone won a jackpot advising all present of one customer's good fortune. Relaxing, I continued through the rows of machines to a cluster of deep leather padded armchairs facing a wire ball. So this was the *Keno* I'd seen on all the signs along Fremont Street. I noticed that to avoid the game getting out of hand, they had placed a conservative limit on the amount of money which was allowed to be bet at each spinning of the wire ball. With the limit imposed you could only buy three light aeroplanes.

One table was shaped as a semi-circle. A man was issuing cards to a group in front of him at machine-gun rate. When he finished he would collect all the money except one lucky person, and place it all over a slot in the table at his elbow. The last the players would see of the bills was when he pushed them into the slot with a plastic rectangle which formerly had been in the hole. The money would somehow finish up in a counting room above, I was told, and was handled by a rubber-tyred front-end loader. Each player at the roulette wheels had devised a magic system for winning but none of them seemed to work. The systems ranged from polishing the marbles on the sides of their noses to breathing on their fingers before clicking them.

I came upon a red-eyed lady of about eighty and I stood beside her watching her feeding coins into a machine. She was very persistent so I asked her how long she had been there before I had come along. Without looking at me or even missing a beat with her chewing gum she said 'three days.' She had hit a jackpot; winning seven shovels full of nickels and was giving them all back. She admitted she grew weary about four o'clock every morning but after a shower and hamburger—which she could get right here in the casino—she was as good as new to press on. Just then the machine itself gave up the fight at last and broke down. In an instant a girl in a swimsuit materialised out of the crowd and after a glance at the number on the machine said into a microphone 'Three-seventeen, mechanical.' In another heartbeat a man was working on the back of the machine with a bag of tools. He soon swivelled it around once more to test the repair with a nickel out of his pocket. As he was advising the elderly lady it was O.K., he was shoved out of the way and she set about feverishly trying to make up for lost time. I asked her who brought her rations but she was oblivious to all but the machine.

I thought a man quietly talking to another machine had finally 'flipped', a term I understood to mean that he needed to see his analyst, so I went over to a gun-belted gorilla and helpfully mentioned it. To my surprise the fellow started laughing and during another outburst he slapped my back with a great hairy paw which sent me face first into a green-lined horse trough. It was explained to me that this particular machine was *supposed* to be talked to. You told it how much you could afford to lose and when that figure was reached it refused to play with you any further.

A S I struggled up out of the trough I saw that it was in fact a table with sides to it and, gripping the edges for support, I somehow dislodged stacks of silver dollars from their neat piles. I was all but buried in the river of money. Looking up sheepishly I came face to face with a lady wearing a clinging crimson gown with lips to match, leaning over the table where she had been screeching something about 'seven' before I interrupted. She asked if I was O.K. in a deep full-throated voice while helping me out of the coins. This made my face the colour of the gown, I knew, because I could feel it. The person in charge of this bathtub began to rake up the mess with a miniature road grader on a stick as I glanced around to see the gorilla about to burst a blood vessel.

I made my exit after that and soon I was in another casino. I saw another gun belt around a hunk of granite employed by the establishment to save people from getting ideas with all this money about. The guard came to me and asked pleasantly if I'd had a flutter on a fruit machine yet. I told him that I hadn't as I'd just had my dinner and couldn't eat another thing. I must have sounded convincing as his jaw dropped and he said 'You gotta be kidding' and slowly walked away on his rounds. Soon, he came back to me and pleaded 'Please say you was kidding,' and he sobbed that his doll would think he'd gone nuts when he told her. That prompted me to mention that he seemed a little old to be playing with dolls, and that in Australia only little girls of four had them. I felt sorry for him as I walked off to overhear him blubbering to another hairy colleague: 'Lefty, only an hour ago there I was carefree and happy,' he whimpered, 'then I got to askin' this guy...'

'You're still too old for dolls.'

In the *Bingo Club*, sporting a model of a gold prospector with a dish of nuggets over the doors, I got talking to another gunman. He asked how my luck was going and when I told him that I didn't gamble, I found out how emotional these people really were. His voice trembled when he asked why had I ever come to Las Vegas. After I told him that I'd never heard of Las Vegas until a few days ago, I reckoned it was about time I left. They could undoubtedly handle trouble but I seemed to be something else again.

I got into a cab and asked the driver to take me to *The Stardust*. He immediately started to tell me how the junkies use snow and that he'd taken a lush to *Frisco* in the 'Caddy' and many other stories, which I'm sure would have been interesting had I known what he was talking about. He went on to tell me how he'd driven Joe E. Brown to LA and was asked to wait for him. A month later Joe ambled out, climbed in and continued on his way. He admitted that there had been times when he had thought Joe had forgotten him, but apart from going for two haircuts, he had stayed with it. At this point I told him that I always cut my own hair. But it was when I asked him what a 'lush' was that he gave a long low whistle and breathed: 'Brother! Wait till I tell my doll.' I thought 'No, not you too,' but said to him brightly: 'I know, she'll figure you've gone nuts.'

When I offered him his tip outside *The Stardust* he pushed it back and sadly asked me to get myself a haircut with the compliments of Vegas.

Outside one place I noticed a crowd of people standing quite still but moving along the footpath at the same time. This place was full of surprises, I decided, as I discovered it was the footpath that was moving. I stood on it and watched the front of the building go by. Soon I found I was a couple of yards away from Mickey Rooney who was presenting a seven-foot man carrying a tray with a prize as he'd just won the 'Waiter of the Week' contest for Las Vegas. It almost broke Mickey's neck talking to him.

Waiting in a line to see the *Patti Page Show*, I became involved in a conversation with a couple in the queue who were on their way back to LA from a holiday in Death Valley. We went in together and ate the chicken dinner required for the admission fee. After another three shows we could just fit into their wagon in which they had offered to drive me back to the *Riviera*.

Another show was under way in the form of two jazz bands which were taking it in turns to entertain the residents, although it was three o'clock in the morning—almost the time the old lady at her machine was getting weary. Billy Williams was singing *Personality* in front of his band so I paused to watch the act. One rather well-fed singer of twenty stone was forced to lie down on a couch after each of his energetically presented renditions of *Won't you come home Bill Williams*. Then Freddy Bell and the Bell Boys took the stage and I remembered having seen him in a picture in Adelaide called *Rock around the Clock* which had nothing to do with

geology. I went over to him and asked him if he could play a song for me which he had sung in the film. Apart from knowing it had something to do with a tired horse, I didn't know its name. He said 'Sure, sure' enthusiastically and turning around to his band yelled out: 'Ding dong for the Aussie, boys.'
I hadn't even told him where I was from.

Later on Billy Williams was chatting to me at a table during his rest period and told me he had been talking to Louis Armstrong about a trip to Australia. Suddenly he grabbed my arm and asked as the whites of his eyes showed brightly:

'Do they really make with the boomerangs over there if they don't like the act?' I suspected that Louis must have been pulling his leg but I assured him that his act would be quite safe. I went on to ask him if his band could play *St. Louis Blues* for me? He was really serious as he said: 'Yeah! 'de boys *know* that one.' I felt as though I'd just asked Sammy Davis if he'd ever heard of *Three blind mice*.

I decided to turn in, it being five o'clock in the morning. I remembered that a Miss Jayne Mansfield was featuring in a show at the Tropicana but I turned in just the same. This sleep was going to cost me a dollar for every ten minutes I was in bed already.

It was the 10th of June and just over a week since I'd left Sydney. Later that morning I found myself on the bus and on my way to the Grand Canyon.

DISCOVERING that Las Vegas was the closest I was going to get to the Grand Canyon, which was only three hundred miles away in Arizona, I had secured a ticket the day before and arranged a visit. As we drove out of Vegas along The Strip I saw that the sheik was still standing on top of *The Dunes* and not paddling his fish hook shoes in the fish bowl full of bikinis.

The driver was good enough to stop at the airport for me to deposit the Gladstone bag under a table, as I'd checked out of the *Riviera*. I then arranged a postponement of my flight to Chicago. The girl at reception fixed it in a minute with a phone call to someone: 'Space in three days, Vegas to Chi, forget Kansas.' I knew I was welcome even before thanking her and we were on our way at seventy miles an hour across Nevada to the Hoover Dam in the air conditioned wagon.

The Hoover Dam, at 726 feet, is the highest in the world holding back the world's largest man-made reservoir. This is a hundred and fifteen miles long and is known as Lake Mead. The mass of concrete is six hundred and sixty feet thick at its base, tapering to forty-five feet thick at the top. The road across the top of the wall is 1,244 feet long. According to the pamphlet, elevators descend into it to a depth of 528 feet or equal to a 44-storey building. It was easier to read all that than carry out my own survey. One side of the dam sits in Nevada, the other in Arizona.

ON the way through Arizona, at a dinner stop, I saw a tall slim-hipped cowboy with a curled-up Stetson and spurs leaning against a hitching rail. I ambled over to find out what sort of bushmen they had out here as he was one of the few people I'd seen *not* wearing a gun. Resting on the rail next to him, careful not to make a sudden move, I asked about his home country and whether he had been to other ranches. I thought for a while that he hadn't heard me but eventually he transferred his weight to his other bowed leg to face me and moved the stalk of grass over to the other corner of his mouth. After studying me for a good minute from under his old dusty hat brim, he sucked in a breath and drawled '*Waal*, son, I generally stick to these here parts, 'cause whenever I git out o' this goldurn Canyon country, I plumb just don't know where I'm at.'

Four Empire State buildings would be needed on top of each other to reach from the Colorado River to the level of the plain above. Why they just didn't say it was a mile deep I don't know. As I went to get out of the bus for a better look, the driver pointed out that, if it were him, he would be getting out of the other side as it was only a step of fourteen inches against the fourteen hundred feet I was about to try. He explained that they quite rightly liked to keep the canyon tidy.

We camped that night in a log cabin called the El Tovar Hotel after the changing colours of the sunset. This pine log cabin had eighty guest rooms. 'Camping' wasn't really the right word.

Everything about the Grand Canyon was amazing. It is 217 miles long and 18 miles wide from its south rim. The two thousand mile-long Colorado River carries the fantastic quantity of half a million tons of suspended silt past any given point every day, and when the sun rises over the Painted Desert, the light slants along it outlining the capes of the opposite rim in gold light, a sight which was to fill the thoughts of the people in the coach for many miles on the way back.

In Vegas, after a six hundred-mile trip, I stood up throughout the entire night watching the shows at the *Riviera*, remembering that last time I hadn't had much use for the room which I didn't bother to book this time.

At six o'clock in the morning as the shows faded away, I walked the four miles along The Strip to the airport, pleased at having left the Gladstone bag there the day before.

I had cause to remember that flight out of Las Vegas. Some months later I read that a man, after losing all he had 'borrowed' from his firm in New York, had blown himself clean out of the aeroplane after take-off, using a home-made bomb. I thought at the time that he just couldn't have told that machine just how much he could lose. I settled down wondering what trouble I was going to get into in Chicago.

Chapter 4

THE SYNDICATE COUNTRY

MASSIVE is a good word to describe Chicago. It is really like any other large city, as long as you see it through a magnifying glass. The Conrad Hilton Hotel, which was to be my home for the next few days, was on the same scale. We had finished the drive from the airport and I walked into the largest hotel in the world, with my shirt under my arm, the Gladstone was again occupying its usual place in a safe box at the airport. At the desk I found that my name was on the register. Following another bell boy up to my room—paying him his salary for carrying my very heavy shirt and still heavier door key—I walked straight out again to launch my attack on the city of syndicates.

On the way out to Michigan Street, through the front doors, I noticed the United Airline office adjoining the hallway. I popped in to check on my flight to Washington. I met Nancy, who told me her name as soon as I walked in. She discovered that I came from Australia and asked me all about it. I started off by explaining I lived in the bush. She asked if it hurt very much. I wasn't sure what she meant, until I realised that she knew a bush only as a scrubby growth, and probably thorny at that. I told her that to us, anywhere away from everything was the bush. She went on to enquire how I cooked food out there in the bush. I said we used a billy. Nancy looked blank at this, so I described it as being a black tin can, with a bent-up bit of wire for a handle and we boil water or porridge in it. By this time the rest of the staff at the counter had joined us. We soon got around to drawing pictures of aborigines and kangaroos on the desk, until one of them mentioned that it was their closing time and she had to catch a bus home. I asked her 'how far?' She said it was a little longer than that. We all seemed to be carrying on conversations of our own for a while. They thought I had said 'half hour?' I didn't know I had an accent until then.

Nancy said she would be walking along Michigan Street to go home, and would be happy to point out things of interest on the way, if I cared to walk along with her. 'By the way,' she added as an afterthought, 'what did you come in for in the first place?' I'd been there for an hour and a half and she handled the booking in ten seconds. 'Space on flight, Chi' to Wash', thirteenth O.K.?' and clicked the phone back on its hook. As we walked north along the street, she pointed out a library which I said looked *beaut* in the paddock across from the Conrad. She was bubbling over with laughter. The well-known friendliness of Chicago people was already being shown.

We had progressed to the intersection of Randolf Street and Michigan Avenue by then, when suddenly a glittering black Cadillac charged out of the cross street and crashed into a new powder blue Buick. I considered the smashing up of these two new cars in front of our eyes nothing short of a catastrophe, and said so to Nancy. She gave it a fleeting glance and continued on with 'Yeah! ... now that's the Prudential Building and over there is the underground car parking area.' We had reached her bus stop.

She called out that she would see me back at the Conrad the next day. I raced back to see the accident.

I dragged myself away to the Prudential Building, for the highest and best view of Chicago, from 601 feet up. All 41 storeys were made of pink granite from Canada The pamphlet explained how the whole thing sits on one hundred and eighty-seven caissons. They were sunk by hand-digging a hundred feet to the same rock strata over which the Niagara Falls flow. The sidewalk outside is warmed by coils set into the concrete to melt away the snow and ice so people won't fall flat on their faces and block the front doorway. The air conditioning removed all particles from the air, I thought I could use that on some of my camps in the bush. The top floor elevators are automatic—and the fastest in the world. The moving stairs are the fastest, and the two top floor moving stairs are the world's highest. The built-in garage is the largest, holding three hundred and fifty cars for the office workers. You can wash the outside of the pneumatically-sealed windows from the inside without hanging about in the wind.

The underground car park opposite, pointed out by Nancy, holds between five and six thousand cars; I immediately thought of the city fathers.

From the top, Lake Michigan looks more like an ocean, over which the wind is always sweeping to give Chicago the name of 'The Windy City'. I never saw a man or woman approach a street intersection without automatically grabbing at their hats or skirts. I could see over to Indiana and Wisconsin. After taking a photograph or two I returned to earth to continue with the hike.

As with Ned Kelly in Australia, a mention of Al Capone must come in somewhere. I found myself outside his unpretentious hotel building, which was a sort of headquarters for his activities. It was growing dark by this time and I could almost hear the rattle of his machine-guns and the exploding of Elliot Ness' bombs. I realised that where I was standing must have been a lively—or deadly—area in those prohibition days.

As I walked away, I noticed a lady struggling with a huge suitcase dragging on the ground. With every few steps she would put it down for a rest. I caught up with her and offered to help, but she declined, saying she was O.K. as she only had four blocks left to her bus stop. Not wanting to appear persistent in this 'Capone country,' I let her go, while I looked at shop windows. Soon I caught up with her again. She was panting louder than ever and I asked if she was sure I couldn't help, whereupon she thought maybe she could use an extra hand after all. I began to tug upwards on the bag handle. She must have been strong to even move it: I almost tore the top out of the bag before it left the ground. It must have weighed a hundredweight. I heaved it along, deciding it was full of sub machine-guns.

She suddenly told me I didn't come from Chicago and guessed I was from Australia. How all these people knew was beyond me. She went on to say—in the usual friendly way of everyone here—that it was a pity I didn't have anyone to show me around. We had travelled a block and a half, so I gently put the bag down for a spell, in case it was only full of hand grenades. My arms felt an inch longer, as they slowly eased out of their sockets. A blast of wind hit us at every corner, cooling the beads of sweat trickling down under my shirt. I heard her say she had just had an idea, 'Say! I gotta pretty daughter.' Hoping that her friendliness didn't get out of hand, I cautiously replied that was nice for her. She pointed out that her daughter would have been happy to show me around, had she been in 'Chi.' Letting out a sigh of relief, I asked where her daughter was at present. Three blocks later, she replied: 'Why honey, she's over in Cincinnati right now arranging the last papers for her divorce.' We had reached her bus stop by then. I thanked her for the thought, and left her with her bag of machine-guns as she called out a cheery 'You're welcome.'

It seemed a good time to seek refuge in my room, if only to let my arms return to their normal length.

The Conrad Hilton used as much water in two days as I did in the making of a mile-long airfield in Australia. Another difference was that I used salty bore water pumped out with a small engine, whereas they could draw on the forty mile-long Lake Michigan. Being the world's largest hotel, the air conditioning pipes, if straightened out, could reach into the stratosphere. The telephone equipment in this one building could serve a town of thirty-five thousand people. If all the carpets were sliced up into two-foot strips, the result would run the full length of Lake Michigan. I imagined that they would be quite upset if anyone decided to prove the point. A fussy person—not wishing to sleep in the same room twice—could still be satisfied if he stayed for seven years. One unique feature was the fact that you could have a proper fire in your room by burning wood. I already had this luxury every day in the bush, so I couldn't help feeling grateful at my constant good fortune. The passenger elevators have travelled five million miles, equivalent to the life of fifty motor cars. So with this in mind I fearlessly stepped into one. I was confident the lift would survive at least another trip up to my room, even though it was on the thirteenth floor.

'…I gotta pretty daughter.'

Next morning, after a night dreaming about machine-guns, divorces and 'Scarface' Al Capone, I gravitated to the coach pick-up point. I had my ticket for a fifty-mile drive around Chicago at the ready. Passing Nancy's office, I received a cheery wave followed by a 'Hi.' One place to see in this city was the Loop. It turned out to be the business and shopping centre. This was, I suppose, 'downtown'. There were hydraulic gutters which rose up out of the centre of the main street, or sank down level again, as required, at the touch of a button somewhere. This controlled peak-hour traffic, turning a two-way street into a one-way. If you had been driving with one pair of wheels on either side of the gutter, just as someone decided to push the button, I could only imagine your car would be sitting on top of it with the wheels spinning in mid-air. It was probably planned with a little more refinement than that, I suspected.

As we passed the mountain of the Wrigley building, I thought of how the G.P.O. was built just to sell stamps.

I was intrigued to see the birthplace of the atomic bomb at the university of Chicago. There wasn't time to inspect Chinatown, or scratch our way through a place with the dubious title of Bug House Square.   So after a last lap past Al Capone's hotel, I returned to the Conrad Hilton. Collecting my shirt from its lone place in the cupboard I caught the coach bound for the airport. While waiting, I told Nancy of my experiences in Chi. Nancy and her happy friends were still laughing as I climbed onto the bus.

During take off the pilot must have discovered something wrong with the aeroplane, so we taxied back for an overhaul. After tea at the terminal, we tried once again and this time we were soon on our way to Washington D.C. It was after dark when the hydraulic gutters fell away behind us.

That put me at my hotel at two o'clock next morning.   I discovered to my surprise that it was the Statler once again.   I could have sworn that I was back in L.A., until I heard there was also one in Texas, St. Louis, Detroit, Cleveland, Buffalo, Hartford, Boston and New York. I was growing a bit tired with all this moving about, so I slept until two o'clock in the afternoon, when I rushed downstairs to the dining room without the encumbrance of the lifts. As I sat, a waitress came over with an armful of menus and enquired if this was to be my breakfast or lunch. Put like that I really didn't know, but told her that we could call it lunch, according to the sun. She gave me a funny sort of look as she selected a menu. It didn't help when I asked her if people were in the habit of having breakfast in the afternoon, in Washington. How then did they get the milking done in time?

I was soon on my way to the needle-shaped Washington monument. I discovered that you could travel to the top of the five hundred and fifty-five foot structure in a lift for a dime. In the line of people waiting to make the ascent, I noticed that I was next to the cutest little girl imaginable, with a flashing smile and ringlets in her hair, ending in white ribbons tied in big bows. Her enormous liquid brown eyes showed the whites when she widened them, as she looked up at the column. She summed up her wonderment at the thought of going to the top in her one word 'Hallelujah!' She then buried her face in her mother's lap, as she hugged her with her little arms, which came out from under the white cuffs of her short-sleeved floral dress.

At the top, the view along Pennsylvania Avenue towards the Capitol Building had to be seen to be believed. To one side was the White House—past a group of baseball diamonds. Court buildings, green lawns and wide streets predominated. Soon I was on my way down to visit these places on the ground.

Lincoln's Memorial had so far been just a photograph in a magazine to me, but on actually entering it and seeing the marble sculpture of the man sitting in his chair, I realised what a work of art it really was. Many times larger than life-size, with details in exact proportion, it made you think you were standing in front of a live being. I knew at last why it had earned world-wide fame.

Outside, there was a long rectangular pool of water. It would cost nothing to go in for a swim, but the bill to enable you to come out would amount to a tidy sum. On the opposite side there was a bridge leading to huge golden figures sitting astride rearing golden horses.

I could see the White House well through the high heavy iron bars of the fence surrounding it. Little animals were eating crumbs on the grass. Someone seemed to have taken Ike's letterbox for a souvenir.

The Capitol Building had the usual solid look about it—like everything else in Washington. From the top of the enormous stairway leading to the front door unfolded the green expanses of lawn of Pennsylvania Avenue. Lincoln's Memorial was on the same line further on. Everything was built with the precision of a carefully-constructed model.

I walked into a museum off Pennsylvania Avenue and ran into the biggest policemen I had ever seen. The bullets from the revolver hanging off his belt would have been capable of passing right through a rhinoceros, let alone a human. I wondered what had happened, or whether he was expecting a rhino soon. He just walked back and forth with his thumb hooked on the gun hammer. He looked aggressively at a frail old lady examining a glass case. I hoped she wouldn't make a sudden move into her handbag for a lace hanky. What did they have in mind when they placed him here in the first place? All I could see was a rope tied to some posts, around the small glass case into which the old lady was looking. Taking my life in my hands, I ambled past him— careful to keep my hands well away from my hunting knife—and in a moment I saw the reason for it all. I found myself one pace away from the world-famous Hope Diamond, the largest on earth. It rested on a silken cushion. It was illuminated by lights flashing like an electric welding rod. I couldn't see what anyone would do with it, assuming they got it past the policeman and took it home. I glanced up to see Frankenstein glaring at me, so after giving him a sickly smile, I wandered away, in my desert boots, with a prickling sensation in the small of my back. If we had had him my camp we could have done away with the bulldozer.

In another place an old-time aeroplane was hanging from the roof on wires. It was so old that it was the first plane in the world, made by the Wright Brothers. Everything here in Washington appeared to be world-class in its field.

Being so close to New York, I began to feel anxious to get there—as any other bushman might. The flight to Manhattan was due to leave late that afternoon. I walked back to the Statler to get my shirt, as that useless Gladstone was in its usual resting place at the airport. Asking the clerk where I could meet the coach, after paying for my sleep in the room, plus the wear and tear on the clothes cupboard, he told me to walk 'All the way along the passage.' I was then to walk 'All the way to the left to the doors.' *All the way* seemed to be peculiar to this city, as I'd heard it nowhere else. After meeting the coach, and driving past the lines of 'sandwich board' pickets, we took off from the airport to fly *all the way* to New York.

Flying over Philadelphia I realised that it was only a fortnight since I'd left Sydney—instead of the age that it felt. There was no time to meditate about this, as the lights of Manhattan were glowing brighter by the minute. Soon the glare of lamps alight in New York City were underneath as we made our landing to the international airport of Idlewild. Being at the southern end of the Queens section of greater New York, the Atlantic Ocean was also in view. In no time we were skimming along the runway after a silky-smooth touch down.

I must have looked like any other hillbilly on his first trip to New York. The terminal buildings were more impressive than the airstrips I had made in Australia: a flour-bag windsock wired to a mulga stick, with a dusty, beaten-up Land Rover to meet the plane taxiing in a cloud of billowing bulldust.

Collecting my Gladstone from the luggage chute, I dragged it over to the safe boxes once again. I opened it for my shirt, got rid of the rest in a cubicle and took out the key. I decided to leave a few dimes inside this time, to cover the time I'd be staying, vowing that I'd never take more than a saddlebag with me next time.

As Greater New York is made up of five areas, I was confused, thinking that Manhattan Island was all there was. Queens, Kings (or Brooklyn), Richmond (or Staten) Island and Bronx are all parts of it, leaving Manhattan as New York City proper. We drove from the airstrip in Queens. At night the lanterns in the skyscrapers had the effect of taking the edge off the gloom. The bus stopped somewhere in all this, and I set off for my hotel, which I guessed, even before checking its name, was *The Statler.*

I was told it was on 7th Avenue at 33rd Street, facing Pennsylvania Station. This was a great help—if I only knew what it all meant—but I walked all the way. Some of the street names looked familiar, as if I had been there before, having heard of them in songs.

As I plodded into the lobby I folded-up the map I had in front of me *all the way*. I waded through the throngs of people at a wedding reception. At the desk I found to my relief that my name was typed in the register. Once again I thanked my friend in the Adelaide airline office, wondering what on earth I would have done if my name hadn't been there. I could probably go out and camp in a big paddock on the map in the middle of the town. I could use my shirt for a pillow. More likely, I would have walked around all night as I had done in Las Vegas.

Trying once again to beat the bell boy to my key, dangling from the fingers of the clerk, I made a grab for it—only to close my fist around thin air. He was far too quick for me, allowing the bell boy to win as he tugged at my shirt in the one action. These boys were professionals. I shrugged, and followed him through the confetti. My room had large letters over the door spelling out the words *Presidential Suite.* I explained that being from Australia, I wasn't even in the running. I mentioned that I could just about get by in an ordinary room. He assured me it was 'O.K. Mac,' and he disappeared ahead of me, doing his stuff, before I had the chance to tell him that my name was Len. I caught the coins for his tip, just before they fell through the hole in my pocket. By the look on his face I couldn't tell what treatment I was in for during my stay here.

There was a long glass-topped table beneath the ivory telephone—which could be used without the trouble of cleaning spiders out—and the bed could be found from the door, as long as you used a compass. The table by the side of the bed was covered with knobs for the push-button radio. You could hardly move in the shower room for accessories. There were felt gloves for polishing your boots, plastic bags for damp undies, a sewing kit with spare buttons and the usual heap of different-sized towels. Selecting one to use for drying my feet, after a wash in another of those flat china things, I made the hike across the room to the large window which opened onto downtown Manhattan. It was a wonderful sight, but I couldn't go to sleep in all that glare, although there were some fancy camp sheets hanging over the windows. Being used to camping in total darkness, I substituted what was there with some blankets and a mat draped over the top.

The sight of the elephant tusk telephone reminded me that I was to make a call to Massachusetts upon arrival in Manhattan. It was to a friend from Woomera who had since married, and had gone there to live. Finding the number—from a letter received in the bush just before leaving my camp—I picked up the handpiece, as late as it was, and gave the operator the number. Within a minute she replied that Mrs June Staley was on the line and to go ahead. It was amazing how all these wires sorted themselves out, to choose June and Ron's phone thirty miles north of Boston. I spoke in a loud voice—being so far away—that it was Len here, yelling from New York. Without hesitation June asked if I could fly up to Boston the next day, where I would be met by her husband Ron, to help him dig for worms the following night. It seemed a long way to go for that, but it appeared that a fishing trip was arranged for me. She asked for my number, which they would ring when they had worked it all out. I pulled the rest of the tusk over to me, and read from the round bit of paper in the middle: *Pennsylvania 6-5000.* It suddenly dawned on me that I'd heard that number before. The sound of it 'rang a bell' as it were, so I mentioned that to them too. She replied 'Sure you have: it was on that Glenn Miller record we had at Woomera.' She added that I was staying at the Statler. I wondered how anyone could remember one telephone number out of the millions here, but she passed it off '*Everyone* knows that one.' So this was where June Allyson had been camping in that movie.

Soon the Pennsylvania 6-5000 phone jangled, causing me to jump a foot. They told me to catch an aeroplane at some airstrip called La Guardia the next day. Ron would be waiting in his station wagon. After thanking her, I realised just how long she had been living in America as she rang off with 'You're welcome.'

Another call was needed so I asked the operator if she had ever heard of La Guardia. I thought 'Oh no, here we go again' when she replied 'Honey you're kidding.' It was after I'd asked whether there were any aeroplanes there that I heard the thump over the earpiece, as she must have fallen on the table and fainted. I suppose it was a bit late and she'd probably had a hard day, so I decided to help her by leaving it for another occasion to ring Andy Axtel.

Chapter 5

THIS IS MANHATTAN –
THAT WAS

THE reason for the unexpected fainting of the operator the night before did not become clear until I had reached the airstrip at La Guardia. I had asked her if she had ever heard of the place and if there happened to be any aeroplanes there. I now understood her slight surprise and hoped she had regained consciousness safely. An aeroplane happened to be landing just as we drove in which I thought was quite a coincidence, but on retracing its flight path back into the sky I could see six more stacked up, patiently waiting their turn to come down. It was like watching a line of children waiting—not so patiently—for their turn at the top of a slippery dip.

I could have bought three pairs of hob-nailed boots with the money I paid *Pennsylvania 6-5000* for the use of their Presidential Suite for five hours, but at the same time I knew that it would have kept the water off had it rained.

The staff at the airline office in Manhattan were just as friendly and happy as they were in Chicago. However, as it was a while yet to knock-off time, I couldn't expect the same individual attention as I had received from Nancy. By the time they had adjusted the date for my onward flight to London and arranged the unforeseen trip to Boston, they were experts on the Australian deserts and knew much more about boomerangs than before. They gave me a blue travelling bag with the compliments of the airline. I saw the initials B.O.A.C. on the side of the bag, as I opened it on the desk to pack my shirt. I knew what they stood for immediately and asked if it was because of all this talk about the desert that I'd be *Better On A Camel.*

Out of the crowd at Boston airport, a man who I had never seen before came over to me and greeted me by name. I thought it must be Ron and wondered how he'd recognised me amongst all these people. He casually told me that his wife June—who was at home with their new baby—had simply informed him what I would be wearing, although we had last met in Woomera six years before. He went on to point out that no one else was wearing a big leather belt with a watch pouch, hunting knife and desert boots. I was forced to agree with him after looking around.

We were soon in his green station wagon driving through Boston. He showed me the points of interest on our way to his house in Chelmsford to the north. I had a letter of introduction to a professor at the Massachusetts Institute of Technology from a friend in Woomera, but after La Guardia I hesitated to ask Ron if he had ever heard of it.

The first thing I was shown as we drove up to his home was a watercolour portrait of an Australian aborigine. It had the desired effect of making me feel at home as it was one I had painted myself and given to June at Woomera. I remembered the very aborigine's camp in the bush were I'd found the subject and it all seemed very far away, which I suppose it was.

During the following three days I saw more rain than I'd seen in the mulga for the past three years. In that time all their friends in Chelmsford had seen the slides of outback Australia from the small box I carried for just such occasions. I was missing the bush more and more with the showing of each slide.

I was asked to go to the supermarket to buy a loaf of bread. Ron was at work and June had to stay at home to look after the new baby. Thinking that nothing could be easier, I set off and after half an hour of searching the shelves, I discovered the bread. An assistant asked what sort of bread I wanted. Having been shown twenty sorts available, from every grain imaginable, I walked back to ask June. Back in the store after obtaining the answer I was then asked which particular sort of rye flour was required. Hiking back to June it was no time before I was at my old place at the bread rack, after which I struggled over to the counter clutching my loaf. I placed it on the stand and turned to see the assistant still where I had left him slowly shaking his head in a most sad kind of way. When I turned around my bread was gone. Electronic rollers had silently eased it away from me and I made a grab for it as I saw it passing the till. I paid the girl on the way yelling to her that all I had wanted in the first place was an ordinary loaf of bread.

The bread was intended for the fishing trip scheduled for the following day. I thought it would be an experience, never having been fishing in the sandhills where I lived. We spent most of the night digging up the lawn for worms which were then threaded into an empty bean can. We had eaten the beans for tea especially so we would have a receptacle for the bait. As we searched, the torch battery faded, causing us to drive to the house of a friend for the loan of a new one. On the way we were delayed by an auction sale under way outside a bankrupt sports store. Ron leapt out of the station wagon and shouted with the rest of the lumberjacketed contestants for the goods on offer. This resulted in his purchase of an extra pair of three-foot long rubber boots for me, a rod, more lines, and a great cane basket for the catch. Under it all was a new torch battery. Midnight saw us still digging out long, slimy worms until the bean can was full. During this operation my precious loaf of bread was being cut up into slices for lunch by June in the warmth of the house. Next morning Ron and I loaded the wagon with ample provisions for an average trip to Alaska. Then we were on our way—not to fish, but to Harriet Mansfield's farm—to collect a fishing licence. This $2.75 card in its plastic waterproof pouch entitled me, as a non-resident alien, to take freshwater fish and saltwater smelt in the waters of New Hampshire for the next three days. I would have been pleased about this if only I had known what on earth they were talking about. I supposed it meant I could keep the fish, including the smelly ones, from New Hampshire.

On the road once more I thought we could at last get on with the fishing. However, the next stop was at the local doctor's place. I could see we still weren't ready, because he had to furnish my blood type to go on the licence. This was probably in case I had to give one of the fish a blood transfusion. It would have been a lot easier to have bought some of the fish I had seen in the supermarket. We were now free to press on with the expedition.

At the river bank I tried to put on the three-foot boots standing up. I hopped about with half of the boot on my right leg. With the other half wrapped around my left ankle, I had to sit down to wrestle with it. I then put on my basket after pinning my licence pouch to my shirt and at last grasped the rod. I saw that Ron had already been fishing for quite a while. To be safe, I took off my watch pouch and hunting knife in case they became moist with the splashing. I pulled a fat worm from the can and spent minutes trying to get it to stay on the hook, as the clove hitch I tied it with kept unravelling. Wading into the water I let the hook drop under the surface, but as I did I thought I noticed the worm slide free again so I pulled it back out to check. Somehow in the time it had been under water, the worm had turned into a ten-inch trout, which was flapping like fury on the end of the line. Both June and Ron realised I had just caught my first fish. I lowered it onto the bank to get it into the basket before it escaped. I then opened the basket in readiness only to find I had June's knitting gear by mistake. Eventually the trout was safely installed and now I had become an angler, I made another cast. I was still waiting an hour later when we were called for lunch, and it seemed my angling days had come to an end as quickly as they had started. Wading back over the smooth rocks under the fast flowing rapids, I stood on a large stone amongst the swirling waters in the slippery rubber boots. I teetered there for several seconds before plunging onto the broad of my back under the river, grabbing at the lid of the basket and rod as I went. Surfacing at last, like a sweating walrus I sloshed in the water-filled boots to the bank to see June and Ron almost as wet from tears of laughter, as they explained the boots were supposed to keep me dry. I pointed out that my fishing licence was dry anyway, and so was my watch which was still lying safely on the bank. I still had the fish after all. It had so far cost three hikes to the supermarket, a midnight auction sale, a night's worm-pulling, a doctor's bill and the licence as well as the galloping consumption I would get from the freezing water. I thought of these things as I poured two gallons of water out of each boot.

Ron had recovered enough by the next day to drive me back to Boston. This was the day we had arranged for the return flight to New York. Ron was still tired as he had lost a lot of sleep from laughing the night before. After saying goodbye to June and the picture of the aborigine, I told her that I hoped she would enjoy my well-earned trout, as I hadn't the time to try it. In any case, if it had been left to me, I would have framed it.

Flying over La Guardia this time, I found I was in one of the planes stacked up waiting to land. Soon after I was dragging myself along Broadway half asleep in the clothes which were drying nicely. Now was the time for me to phone Andy Axtel whom I'd last seen in San Francisco a month before. Calling the number he had written for me in the cab, I was greeted by a most enthusiastic enquiry as to where I was and if it were possible to come on out right away. This came from Mrs Axtel's father who was staying with them and was expecting my call. He soon had it arranged for me to talk with Mrs Axtel at a golf club where she was spending the afternoon with Andy. She thought I'd forgotten to ring and had gone on to London. She advised me to catch a bus from the Port Authority terminal. One dollar's ride would put me on a corner in Newark, New Jersey where her son and daughter would be waiting for me in their yellow convertible. She would describe me to them so I checked to see if the hunting knife was in its place on the belt.

At the terminal on 8th Avenue and 41st Street, a girl stood next to me in the queue. I asked her if I was in the right line for *Noowark:* I was told that it was 'All right already.' This resulted in my having non-stop travel talk on the way as she was going there too. Her name was Patti. During the trip she got out her transistor radio which was soon belting out a loud jazz session. She smiled as she clicked her fingers explaining to me that 'man you gotta be *with* it!' Her eyes were shut as she tapped her foot on the floor of the bus and breathed 'Dig that beat,' to which I answered 'No' and that I was surveying in Australia instead of market gardening. I quickly informed her, as I saw the look on her face, that I thought she'd asked did I 'Dig that beet?'

There was still a queer look in her eyes as the ticket man told me that the next stop was mine, so I took up the blue bag and shirt and farewelled the transistor as my little friend Patti had once more become 'sent.'

Drew Axtel told me I must be Len and I was soon with him and his sister Dale in their convertible. Another couple were also there, and we were on the way to the golf club when I saw something out of the corner of my eye. I spun around to see the boot slowly opening as a great canvas and iron thing emerged to pass right over our heads. I yelled out to duck as I crouched down on the floor of the car and was surprised to hear them all laughing. Drew explained that was why it was called a convertible and he had merely pressed a button on the dash to cause all this to happen. They wanted to hear all about Australia after that, and by the time we had pulled up amongst the Cadillacs and Buicks we were great friends. Carefully stepping around a tiled swimming pool, mindful of the fishing trip the day before, we went into the club rooms where Mrs Axtel hurried over to find Andy. He had just won a silver tray for his golf and was having a banquet with all the members before the presentation. A surgeon friend of theirs joined us and within thirty seconds he had pointed out nine millionaires as he helped to pile up my plate from the heaps of food.

We walked out after the ceremony and I made for the yellow convertible where I'd left my shirt, but Andy asked me to come home with him as that was his son's car. We climbed into a big new Buick which had not felt many desert boots on its carpeted floor. After a smooth drive filled with questions of how I'd survived in the USA on the way over, my yarns about Mason in L.A. and the crying gorillas in Vegas, we finally stopped at a driveway. I could make out the two storey house quite easily, without binoculars. I was informed wild deer were roaming about at the bottom of the yard. The evening—after the convertible had arrived with my shirt—was spent with another colour slide show, using the pictures I had projected to the population in Massachusetts. Quite a gathering from the golf club turned up for it, including the informative surgeon.

Drew offered to accompany me into New York the next day to show me the ropes and Mrs Axtel's father insisted on driving us to the bus stop in his Chevvy. He arranged to be there to meet the late afternoon bus on our return. They were certainly wonderful people, I thought, as we converged once more upon Manhattan. Drew showed me a cathedral capable of holding twenty thousand people. Later I saw 'The Little Church Around the Corner' where they could just squeeze in a minister. Although rain limited our progress we were still able to examine the red dragons dimly lit by candlelight in a Chinese Den. We then moved on to the Port Authority terminal to return to Livingstone. Drew helped by telling me what to look for on the following day's expedition.

The Chevvy was waiting as arranged. We were warned that there was to be a barbecue that night in the bush to make me feel at home. My life in Australia was one long barbecue but this proved to be one with a difference. I was about to volunteer to chop some firewood when they put some black blocks on a disc plough blade held up by three legs and lit a few square inches of paper under them. Within a minute they were grilling meat. Next, out came a small bundle which opened up to a good-sized table complete with seats ready for silver knives and forks on bamboo

Las Vegas.

Las Vegas.

TV antennae on top of Empire State Building, New York.

Empire State Building from 5th Avenue.

Manhattan skyline.

Piccadilly Circus.

Clock Tower, Houses of Parliament.

"...and at Woomera they get to the size of weather balloons." The author (right) describing Australian onions to Sir William Penney.

The author at Land's End...almost "Beadell's End."

Gypsy boy with long-eared dog, Eire.

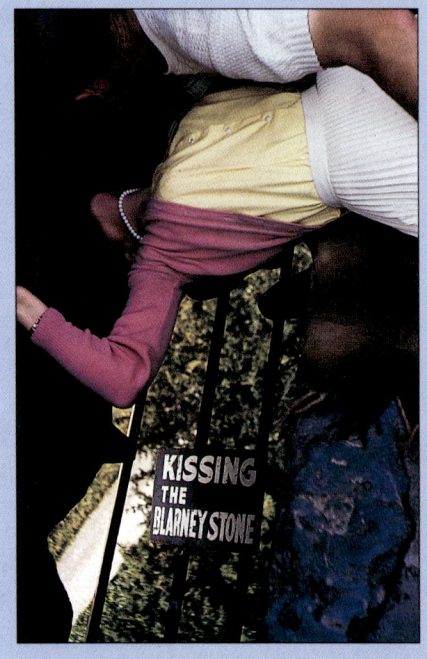

Kissing the Blarney Stone.

Orange Day parade, Londonderry.

Edinburgh Castle.

Maureen and Mary at King Arthur's Seat, Edinburgh.

Princes Street from Edinburgh Castle.

Theodolite repairs, Cooke, Troughton & Simms, York.

mats. There were no clouds of flies as Mrs Axtel served out the food on coloured throw-away plates, after she had hung up her P.V.C. grip-on apron. I had the most homely tea since leaving the bush. Dale and Drew switched on a portable television set and as we ate I thought that at last I had found an easier way of living to the only one I knew.

Andy was due to fly to Chicago in the morning to see to one of his establishments which made automatic arc welding machines. He was a busy fellow and was looking into the idea of opening another place in Las Vegas. He also turned out to be the mayor of Livingstone. I remembered the plane trip to Hawaii where we had met and the cab ride to the hotel in San Francisco which had resulted in my being here right now. So, with the same friendly arrangement with the Chevvy, I plunged once again into Manhattan, this time on my own.

MY first plan was to circumnavigate the island. To do this I had to somehow get to Pier 83 at West 43rd Street. As explained by the Axtels, all the avenues, such as Park, Madison and 5th Avenue lay north-south, and all the streets travelled east-west. Fifth Avenue is a sort of centre line where West 42nd Street turns into East 42nd Street, and the numbering of the streets increases as you progress north. The Avenue numbers increase as you go west. I would have liked to have had my prismatic compass with me, I thought, as I stood at the intersection of 42nd Street and 3rd Avenue. Now all I had to do was to hike north to 43rd Street then west along East 43rd Street, to 5th Avenue where it should turn into West 43rd Street and continue along to catch the boat.

The boat sailed counterclockwise around the island. After we started going south, Manhattan was to the east of us. I noticed a rather high shed which I was told was the Empire State Building, the tallest building in the world. No wonder it seemed big to me even though I had seen the biggest windmill tower in the Northern Territory. I knew then what my first call would be once back on the island. I then saw a most untidy looking parking area, which was obviously too small, as the cars were parked one on top of the other to a depth of eight vehicles. I wondered how the owners of the ones on the bottom were supposed to drive off, as there didn't appear to be a crane handy. Some cars had been shoved off altogether and were half submerged in the Hudson River. Perhaps their owners were only charged half rates.

Further on I floated past Liberty Island where the famous statue stood. In comparison, the humans at its base looked like bull ants. I remembered having been told that Eiffel—who designed the Eiffel Tower—also created the Statue of Liberty.

A loudspeaker advised us that we were sailing under the Brooklyn and Manhattan Bridges. Henry Hudson discovered the island in 1609, calling the river after himself. Then old Peter with two shiploads of Dutchmen came along in 1626 to buy the island from the Indians. The Indians wanted thirty dollars' worth of the trinkets the double Dutchmen were offering. But they were beaten down to twenty-four dollars; it would have been cheap at twice the price. The transaction was completed when the Indians said 'Orlrightie.' It wasn't nearly as complicated as it would have been today, but still, everyone was happy. The loudspeaker droned on to inform us that the Duke of York came along thirty-eight years later. He told the Dutchmen he would fight them for Manhattan. He must have won because he changed the name from New Amsterdam to New York. The Dutch were down twenty-four dollars and no island, so they came back nine years later in 1673. They won it back in a fight, changing its name once more, this time to New Orange. It wasn't until after it had gone back to the English a year later that the Indians started to get a bit confused. For a while they didn't know who to pay their rates to. When it turned back into New York they at last had an address. Everyone agreed on one thing: that it was *New*. The Indians were satisfied as they not only had their twenty-four dollars, but they had much more in entertainment. Only six years after Captain Cook had discovered that Sydney would be an ideal site for a bridge, George Washington managed to get his hatchet through the customs in 1776 and Manhattan then became a battleground. As far as I could see it had been nothing else ever since old Peter Minuit first bought the place.

All this brought us past the City Hospital, built on the appropriately-named Welfare Island in the East River. We were soon sailing between New York and the Bronx along the Harlem River.

As soon as we landed at the western end of 43rd Street I headed off to find the Empire State Building. I had it all worked out to walk east along West 43rd Street and cut south down Broadway to West 34th Street where I could walk east until it changed into East 34th Street. I would then be at 5th Avenue. Right there, according to my calculations, should be the tallest building in the world. I stopped periodically to observe the sun for direction as I hiked with my yard-square map of New York out in front of me. People about me were also interested in the sun as they often stopped to stare with me up into the sky, until one man wearing a yellow hat with an eight-inch brim asked me what I was looking at. When I told him I was looking at the sun to find north he became visibly relieved as he said 'Yeah now I get it; for a while there I thought you was some kind of a nut.' His footsteps stopped suddenly soon after, and I looked around to see him staring at the sidewalk as he scratched his head holding the yellow hat between his fingernails. He half turned, shrugged his shoulders helplessly and walked on. He certainly seemed to be acting in a most peculiar fashion.

I was going well until I reached Times Square, still with the map out in front of me. I stopped myself just in time from continuing south along 7th Avenue. I felt I was drawing nearer my target as I relocated Broadway and pressed on south to get to West 34th Street where I had to turn east. I was glad of that bush survey experience back home in Australia.

With my face still buried in the map I ended up on 5th Avenue…but where was the building? I couldn't see it anywhere. I went over and asked a great big shiny lawman, with a stag horn butt on his heavy revolver, if he could tell me where the Empire State Building was, or had it been moved since the boat ride? His reply didn't seem to make sense to me as he merely described me as being a 'wise guy.' I thanked him but pointed out that although I'd got here by means of the sun it wasn't all that clever, because after all, I still had the map. There was something funny about this man as he only narrowed his eyes and belligerently hooked his thumb around the gun hammer. Just as I was thinking that I was back in Arizona, he spun around and roared off into the traffic on his three-wheeler bike, his siren wailing. The next people I asked were a happy-looking couple, but as I finished pointing down at the map, I saw that the girl had unhooked her arm from her friend's and was hiding behind him. They seemed to be a scary lot hereabouts. He laughed as he said: 'For gosh sakes, stop looking down at that there map and try looking up for a change.' Copying the Indians I said 'Orlrightie' whereupon I could at last see a reason for everyone's unusual behaviour, as I stared up at the building rearing into the sky for a quarter of a mile. I knew it was that high because it was a quarter of the depth of the mile-deep Grand Canyon. By this they imagined me to be something of a newcomer to New York, causing the girl to come out of hiding. I told them about the policeman and could hear them laughing to the end of the block.

'Where's the Empire State Building?'

A visibility chart was in the room where the queue entered the building. The chart showed just how clear it was from the top at that moment. Its range went from infinity to zero, according to the cloud cover or rain. It was currently showing forty miles. I paid my dollar and was soon in the elevator going up at fifteen miles per hour to see what was described as the world's most spectacular view.

It took a minute to get there, with a change of elevators. From the top of a hundred and two storeys, in the heart of Manhattan, I was more than willing to agree with the other sixteen million people that the view alone was worth a trip to New York. I would have liked to have had with me one of my desert aboriginal friends, who had never been higher than the nearest sandhill. I could understand exactly how he would have felt because I was feeling the same. On top of the building was a television tower equivalent to another twenty-two storeys. I've heard of workmen receiving 'height money' for jobs in precarious places: these must have put in regularly for 'angel money.' The overall height was thus brought to one thousand four hundred and seventy-two feet. In case no one had ever thought of taking photographs from the fence around the viewer's platform, I set-to and took a few of my own, although I couldn't get rid of the feeling that perhaps someone had done the same before. I subsequently showed the resulting slides to many groups of natives at aboriginal missions and cattle stations, on a screen made by hanging a tent fly between two trees, with a line-up of truck batteries and *trannies* as I was told they were called, for power to the projector. These slides brought no reaction whatsoever but when I showed images of some baboons from Tanganyika, they made the ranges and dunes ring with their yelling.

I started back down again after I'd finished. As we dropped down the shaft encasing the elevator, I shuddered to think how that engine from the bomber aeroplane had done the same thing. I remembered hearing how the plane flying blind in a fog amongst the skyscrapers had crashed into the Empire State Building two thirds of the way up. One of its engines had kept on going into the offices, and down the shaft. I imagined the typist sitting there at her desk when a stray engine had come in through the window—although it was shut—shifted the carriage on her typewriter on its way past, and on out through the closed door. All her sheets of good typing paper would have been scattered everywhere in the draft. What a shemozzle!

Lying on my back on the footpath in 5th Avenue, I was able to secure a picture looking up at the building without having my neck dislocated. Funnily enough, no one took a second look at this operation, whereas the map episode caused a near riot.

Later on I saw someone doing the very same thing down on The Bowery, but he didn't have a camera. His head was hanging down into the gutter causing his neck to arc back at right angles, as the rest of him was across the footpath. The grimy black rags he wore made an interesting comparison with the shiny black Cadillac parked alongside his cheek. As I was about to alter his position, in case the Caddy chose to drive off and dent his head, another man nearby was gradually sliding down a lamp post. Before he joined his friend I heard him ask, as he pointed in the general direction of the car, whether he could spare the time to drive him to Grand Central. Further on, as I was passing a shop, another man came rolling slowly out of the door like a log of wood. I waited as he rolled right on past me and into the gutter where he dropped the last foot into a pile of trash. I went over to him but he was sleeping like a log, to use an apt euphemism. It would have been a shame to disturb him. A few more paces on there was another man quite busy shrieking at the top of his voice in the middle of a side alley. He was ripping what was left of his shirt into tiny fragments and, as he was occupied, I left him alone. I got to thinking that *here* was a place with a difference.

From there on I was stepping over bodies lying at all angles on the concrete and not one of them was taking photographs. Although it seemed odd at first, I concluded that they wouldn't have been lying about like driftwood unless they wanted to. They had the added advantage of being able to roll down into the Chinese den when it rained, without even getting up. I saw one lady huddled in a doorway, opening onto the footpath, where she lived all the time in the employ of the tourist bus line, to be pointed at by visitors as an attraction. She wasn't badly-off, because the door would shield her from the cold easterlies which blow in from the Atlantic.

A long-haired barefooted man in ragged half-length trousers, a huge brown coat, wearing a scraggy beard and altogether looking like Robinson Crusoe told me that I was in Greenwich Village. He was stooped, clutching an easel with drawing board under one arm, a female figure under the other, trudging to somewhere or other. I imagined I was suddenly in Calcutta instead of within sight of Wall Street.

AFTER inspecting Wall Street, where there was probably more money stacked than anywhere else in the world, next to an area the same size where there was no money *at all*, I rode on a bus north to Harlem. On the way I saw a paddock in the middle of all this activity with a few waterholes in it. It could have quite easily run a herd of milking cows but none were to be seen. Mentioning this to the Axtels that night, I gathered it was known as Central Park.

The bus to New Jersey was ready to leave by the time I'd found the Port Authority terminal. The sun had gone behind a bank of clouds and fog was rolling in, causing me to race north along Park Avenue from East 42nd Street. With little time to spare, I backtracked after reading the street sign, then headed south to 41st Street. This second delay in the fog compelled me to go west to 8th Avenue where I slumped into the waiting bus a minute before it took off. I had to meet the Chevvy at all costs. Andy had returned by this time from Chicago and joined in the audience, which persisted in laughing all the time, instead of listening to my travel talks of the day. The London-bound plane was due to take off from Idlewild at dusk the next night so I realised sadly this was to be my last evening with this most wonderful family.

Thanking them for their great kindness the next morning, and promising to write if I lived to get back to Australia, I unexpectedly found I was able to do something for them in return. Andy asked me if I would call in to see his father who lived in

Melbourne and give him the latest first-hand news of his son and family. I assured him I would, and that Christmas when I drove through Melbourne with some children from Woomera, I did just that. He had been delighted to hear the news and we wrote a combined letter there and then to Andy at Livingstone, New Jersey. Mrs Axtel drove me to the bus that morning in the yellow convertible, as the Chevvy had driven off to Chicago where her father lived.

MAKING my way to Times Square I stood watching the scene at one of the most well-known spots in the world. There was a waterfall nearby where thousands of gallons of water gushed down a sloping mountainside advertising something cool. Standing where I was, by a doorway, a man came out of the shop and asked me if I wanted to buy something for my doll. I told him I didn't have a doll but he guided me inside nevertheless and showed me a radio capable of receiving programmes from Hong Kong. When I told him I didn't need a radio which did that, as I couldn't understand Chinese, he took out a necklace saying he'd throw that in as well.

He grabbed a twenty dollar bill from my hand which he'd asked to see, and promised that if I added another hundred to it he'd give me the first two items, as well as another radio which worked off the sun. I assured him that I never wanted to listen to a radio in the sun as it was mostly over the century where I came from. He spent the next half hour trying to sell me four earrings. I pointed out to him that I didn't know anyone with four ears. Even after he'd given up I had to jump the counter to get my twenty dollars back. I suspect I was probably the only failure he'd ever had and it hurt his ego.

The airline coach arrived at Idlewild in heavy fog. By the time I'd found my safe box containing that stupid Gladstone bag, it was very nearly time for take off, through a gate in another building quite a distance away. I found to my dismay that the lock had been sealed and I was unable to open it with my key, so I raced over to the desk. An attendant came back with me but refused to open it until I had given him two bits. I asked him what he would like two bits of, and when his jaw dropped open I gave him a quarter, and told him to buy them for himself. It was raining by this time so I jammed the shirt and blue bag into the Gladstone, which I hoisted to my shoulder. I ran through the drizzle to the luggage checking desk.

Panting like a tired sheep dog, and soaking wet—apart from the one dry shoulder—I heard the speaker announcing that due to the heavy fog my 510 Comet 4 flight to London was being held up for a while. Checking the bag over the counter, I discovered the visibility was barely a hundred yards, but if it lengthened another fifty we could take off. In that way the pilot could see a couple of runway lights at a time and drive between them. They asked me to wait for a call so, in my best American, I replied 'Orlrightie' and sat down feeling now more like a dripping water spaniel than a sheep dog.

The call came about the time the puddle of water around my feet equalled the volume from an upset billy can. As the call was repeated I told the speaker 'All right already.' Soon afterwards I was being hurtled past the runway lights towards London on my first jet plane ride.

Chapter 6

THE FOG CLEARS

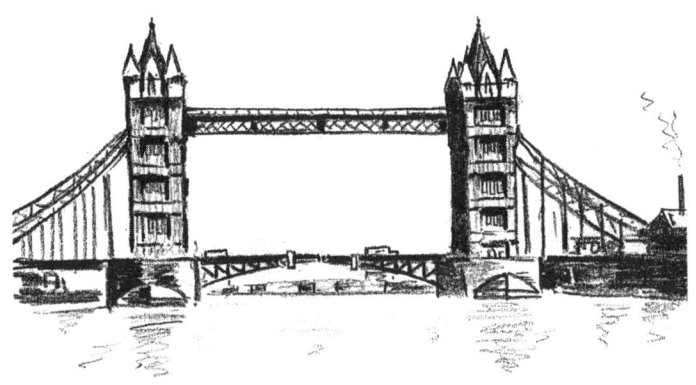

E VEN through the accumulation of black grit on the glass, the bright colours of the picture hanging on a wall at London airport could still be seen. It represented the brightest spot in the place, and provided me with my first impression of England, reproduced as it was, with great emphasis on detail. It made an altogether most attractive decoration. It was the subject of the picture, however, which seemed to me to be a little odd. At the sight of a man with bucket and broom I had an idea. I told him I had just come from New York, and asked if we had veered a trifle south in the fog and landed in Italy by mistake? He must have been a dummy as all he said was 'Cor,' as he hurried off. It had nothing to do with apples. I knew by this time that we were in England all right, but why ever did they choose a colour enlargement of a plate of mixed up spaghetti as a picture in the airport? The girl with the peaches-and-cream complexion at the desk replied to my observation about the picture, that it was certainly a clever idea. That framed map of London streets had helped many newcomers.

We had arrived at London airport in a dense fog after a 'talked down' instrument landing, during which all I could think of was cabbage patches. I had occupied a seat next to an actor from California on his way to take part in T.V. films in the U.K. The coffee on the flight had been too strong for me, so I had emptied all my envelopes of sugar into it. The rank taste was still there, so the actor had given me his lot. Still no good, I obtained more from the hostess who came along as I was pouring in my eleventh envelope. She asked him if he also wanted more. He replied over my pile of empty packets that just watching me was enough for him.

The plump girl at the desk proved to be wonderful at finding a place for me to stay. The first night was to be at Gloucester Road. She also arranged a call for me to Hastings where John Foreman, a colonel who had just left our atomic testing ground at Maralinga, lived. He had asked me to contact him as soon as I landed in England. We arranged over the phone that I would travel by train the following day to St. Leonards-on-Sea, and stay with him for a few days to get settled.

This meant carrying that old Gladstone bag with me for the first time on this trip. After changing a twenty dollar bill into sterling, I shouldered my bag and trudged out into the rain. It was the twenty I had fought the shopkeeper in Times Square for only the day before. I saw a little black car which had no passenger door and no seat, but in its place a huge leather seat belt about the size of a surcingle on a pack saddle. As I stood there thinking that a passenger would keep dry only if the rain were falling vertically, and how cold he would feel in the winter, the driver called out and asked if I wanted 'A cab, Guv?' So this was a London taxi! It turned out the passenger seat was a place to put your Gladstone bag. It was strapped in with the surcingle and you sat in the back seat out of the rain. This arrangement allows you to watch your luggage being gradually soaked to pulp in the front.

I gave him the address at Gloucester Road supplied by the girl at the desk. We sloshed away from the air terminal. It was mid-morning when we pulled up outside an establishment with the front door facing a paddock surrounded by a spiked, heavy iron fence. That grass must have been valuable. My room was so small that I had to open my bag in the hall in order to get my shirt out. This saved hanging from the cupboard door to do the same thing with the Gladstone on the bed; there was no room on the floor. With the bag safely inside I found one of us had to move out, so I

went down the narrow staircase to ask the landlady how I could get to Australia House, as there might be some mail there for me. She told me if I caught the tube at Gloucester Road to Temple I'd be almost there, concluding that I was to bring no lady friends back with me. I wondered what she was talking about as that room couldn't hold a pet dog. As it was I'd have to camp with the bag tied to the door knob.

I was still wondering what she meant as I walked outside under the shelter of some overhanging trees in the paddock. I headed towards the tube station called Gloucester Road.

Emerging to the surface at Temple, like a jack rabbit from a burrow, I was soon installed in the friendly atmosphere of Australia House, reading some letters from home. One of them was from Frank Kennedy of the *Adelaide Advertiser*, enclosing an article concerning me. It had been printed since I'd left and featured the recent desert survey project I had been on, including a photograph of me. Going to the folder of Adelaide papers, I looked for the edition with the article. As I was reading it a man came to stand next to me: he was waiting to read the same papers. As I handed them over I asked if he knew the person shown in the photograph. He looked from me to it then back again and exclaimed, after he'd shut his mouth which had been hanging open, that it was me. It seemed amazing that here we were, two South Australians in London reading a newspaper story about one of us twelve thousand miles from where it was printed three weeks before.

The bank nearby was supposed to have some money for me arranged by my friend Robbie the manager at the Salisbury branch, so I went in to see if I could get it out. Sure enough, good old Robbie had done a life-saving job although the amount had shrunk considerably to sterling values. I drew it all out and pushed it into a kangaroo skin bag I'd made for the purpose. Having the rest of the day free I set off through the streets towards our Woomera H.Q. in Castlewood House on Oxford Street, guided by another map carried well out in front of me. I still couldn't help thinking that it looked like a plate of spaghetti. In an extension of Oxford Street called High Holborn I noticed a bag shop, so I went in to look over their wares. I asked the little man who shuffled over if he would trade in a solid leather and brass horse-and-cart bag for a smaller one. I explained I had just come from Australia and the Gladstone was too big for my shirt. He looked at me over his pince-nez glasses in a funny kind of way, but agreed he would. I selected one and advised him I'd be back in the morning with the Gladstone just after milking time, and continued to walk west to Oxford Street. It was there I almost crashed into Harry Higgs who was running as fast as he could towards me. The last time I'd seen Harry was in my camp at the Coober Pedy Opal Fields in

South Australia He was now doing a spell representing Australia at a London office. His red wire moustache was bristling with the exertion as I said 'How're you getting along Harry?' When he recognised me he all but bit the moustache clean off. He told me he had to cash a cheque a long way away before closing time. With the weekend upon us I cashed it for him there and then, with Robbie's money from the bank. I could fix it up with more time to spare later. Us Aussies had to stick together.

This led to my having tea with Harry at his home near Richmond Park. The one thing his small son Rowland insisted I draw for him was a 'Foul Fiend.' With the train trip to Hastings already arranged, but with an invitation for a future meeting with the Higgs family, I caught a tube train back to Gloucester Road to relocate my room. Passing the landlady's cubicle I saw she noted with satisfaction that I was on my own. As I eased up the stairs, breathed in, climbed over the Gladstone, and squeezed between a small table with a jug on it I made an interesting manoeuvre sideways to get up onto the bed. Once there I could take off the desert boots for the first time since I'd put them on at Andy Axtel's place in New Jersey the day before. I felt a little sorry as I looked at the Gladstone bag which my father had owned and I'd known since I was six years old, realising that it and I were to part company in the morning at High Holborn. I switched the dim light bulb off and went to sleep, wondering what the jug was for.

Struggling past the iron caged-in paddock the next day, with the bag on my shoulder, I knew I had to get to the bag shop before catching the train to Hastings. There was no time to lose. With the booklet of the London tube system, which made the Thames look more like an air conditioning duct than a river, I saw a blue line joining Gloucester Road to Holborn passing under Piccadilly Circus. Dragging the bag down into the hole in the road leading to the train line, I soon surfaced at Holborn, where I was surprised to see that the fog had cleared. The sun was shining in a clear blue sky. That was how it remained for the following two months and I was told by everyone that it was the longest, hottest and driest summer they had recorded for two hundred years. It was almost as if the stored-up heat I'd brought, from twenty years in Central Australia, had been too much for this climate and it had warmed it up for them. I in turn had been looking forward to seeing some rain. It was surely too strange to be a coincidence as I'd only arrived there the day before. I told everyone that I was only too pleased to help, feeling like an aboriginal rainmaker in reverse.

I asked a uniformed railway porter where this High Holborn was, whereby he looked at me blankly until I showed him the map. His face lit up and he burst out with 'Cor! you mean 'Igh 'Ob'n,' and soon I was recognising landmarks which pointed to the bag shop. The doors had not yet opened, so I sat on the Gladstone waiting on the footpath. People stared like they had never seen anyone wearing desert boots and a hunting knife, sitting on a Gladstone before in 'Igh 'Ob'n. Finally the owner arrived at ten seconds before nine o'clock, remembered me, and I followed him inside.

He carefully examined the bag inside and out after which I told him it was worth at least a pound. He offered me only a 'nicker' for it, whatever that was. With that he gave me the bag I'd selected the day before. Sitting on the floor I transferred the shirt, shorts and blue airline bag from the Gladstone into the new one. I paid him the difference to complete the transaction. I slowly and sadly walked out of the shop as it hit me that no longer would the Gladstone occupy its rightful place in a horse-drawn buggy or be shifted from one safe box to the next in US airports.

The train was due to leave at a place called Charing Cross near the 'air conditioning duct' river shortly, so I had to hurry. It was easy to find on my map. The sun was out and it was a pleasant stroll, passing some waterholes on the way. There was a statue of a man on top of a high column, probably out of reach of the many pigeons about. When the train drew into St. Leonards-on-Sea, I took up my new bag and saw John waiting outside with his car. He had asked me to draw a picture for his small daughter to send to her from Maralinga. I knew the name of the little girl who came to meet me and said 'You must be Lindsay.'

At his place his wife informed me that there was H. and C. in the room I would be using. I was shown around and couldn't see any horses and cows and asked where they were. She said it was the temperature of the water laid on to the basin that she had been referring to. I could see I had a lot to get used to and with that we went downstairs to prepare for the trip out to Pevensey to see my first castle.

It had cannon balls for *the enemy*, slots in the walls so they could fire arrows at *the enemy*, and a moat to keep *the enemy* away in the first place. It seemed a lot of work just to settle some difference of opinion with someone, but it was the oldest structure I had ever seen. Anything put up sixty years ago was old in Australia and this was built donkey's years ago. There was no sign of bush hospitality in the design and I wondered who all these enemies were. They didn't seem to have any friends at all. No spare rooms for visitors; just cannon balls.

John came to see me in the morning after Lindsay had brought along a mug of tea. Before I had time to arise, he informed me that he'd seen a car for hire at a garage he knew a chain away from his home. He'd already advised the owner that I was on the look out for one to use during my stay in England, so we went down to see it. Soon the arrangements were made for its hire for over two months. It was a black Vauxhall with a white top. It even had a radio installed. On checking with the police, I found that the driving licence I used on the Nullarbor Plain in Australia worked for up to a year in the UK, despite the fact that Piccadilly Circus would be a bit different to the bush. I was to drive that car for five thousand miles before returning it in September.

William the Conqueror had a terrible row with some enemies at a town called Battle, not far from where we were, in 1066. So we drove over to see the place while the car was being checked. I saw where somebody had looked up to see if it was going to rain, and got an arrow in his eye. It made it so sore that it was his tombstone I stood looking at on the spot. That was just outside Battle Abbey, and it was there it occurred to me that William and I were going to attack England from the same spot. The only battle I had at Hastings was to leave the kind hospitality of the Foreman family the next morning, as I drove forth like a knight in a shining Vauxhall.

The first journey planned was east to Dover to locate an address given to me by Nell Mott, a friend from Woomera. Her sister Betty lived there with her husband Major Bob Genn at the Old Park army barracks. I found their house, which looked out over the Channel to France. As I stood there thinking of the swimmers who tackle that crossing, the door opened and I heard my name being called to come on in. Nell had posted the newspaper clipping to them. They had been expecting me, recognising me from the photo. They proved to be wonderful people with their children Helen, Margaret and Ross, who immediately handed me a pencil and school book and ordered me to draw a kangaroo for them. I was forced to use the front door as a desk and do it before being allowed to enter. Early in the conversation it was revealed that both Betty and Nell had sheltered in my cousin's homestead on his cattle station in Queensland, flood-bound by the Burdekin River, thirty years before. Little did they think they would be repaying old Jim Atkinson for his help so long afterwards in this way twelve thousand miles removed. I hoped that Jim had treated them better than the landlord of Pevensey did his visitors.

The next morning we all went for a drive to Canterbury Cathedral which I'd heard so much about. While there I noticed the statues both lying down and standing had one thing in common. They all had their noses knocked off. I remarked about this to Bob who told me that Oliver Cromwell was responsible. Anything he didn't like he took it out on the statue's nose, probably as a result of something that had happened to him in his boyhood. The ones standing up were operated upon with a battle axe whereas the horizontal ones would have responded better to a golf club. He must have had many grievances as there were dozens of noseless statues about as a result of jolly old Oliver's work.

The afternoon saw us all attending an official rifle shoot at the range. A young soldier recruit wearing squeaking black hob-nailed boots rushed up to me, stood stiffly to attention and enquired 'I say, would you care for a seat,...SUH?' The 'sir' was shouted at the top of his high voice and gave me quite a start, but I thanked him and asked his name. 'Private Polkinghorne,...SUH!'

I was ready for him this time as he turned left with a click of his gleaming boots, which nearly threw his knee out of joint and marched off to fetch the chair. I then sat in the middle of the prairie watching from an armchair. At the end a group came over to me and asked my opinion of how they went. I told them they were just great and soon would be as good as one old bushman I knew in Australia. They were immediately interested so I repeated the old fable of the expert with the Winchester. This man could hit that two hundred-yard target smack in the bull with his sights set at a hundred yards. They were all sitting on the grass staring up at me as I asked if they could see the rock protruding out of the ground half way to the target. When they had all seen it I went on '...and if he were here he'd do it by bouncing the bullets off that.' The timely arrival of Bob saved me as Private Polkinghorne burst out with 'I say chaps what a jolly good show,' and turning to me asked as he held out his rifle: 'Look here Sir, but would you mind awfully showing us how he did it?'

Later, we saw a concrete aeroplane commemorating the spot where the first cross Channel flight had landed. As it was to be found in the grass half way up a steep hill, I gathered that it hadn't been an altogether organised landing. A look through Dover Castle followed and I discovered that the Normans had made this one complete with the slots for *the enemy*. These ancients must have hated one another.

On the way back to London, after leaving Dover where I assured the Genns I'd call again when I returned the car, I stopped at a friend's house in Kent. That was the day I saw Sir Winston Churchill at his Chartwell home. After a drive around Bromley we stopped outside a high rock fence. Through the gates we saw a large expanse of lawn with a policeman's head lying by a shrub. It still wore its helmet. As I was thinking what an odd ornament Sir Winston had chosen, it blinked its eyes at me. I blinked right back and to my surprise a neck followed by a pair of blue shoulders rose out of the ground. My friends directed my attention to the solid stone house, and to one window in particular, where I saw Sir

Winston Churchill. I wondered if he would like to hear about the kangaroos first-hand, but as I glanced back the head was now staring at the hunting knife on my belt and scowling darkly, so I decided to delay the interview. It was really only a penknife in a pouch but to him it would have taken on the appearance of at least an assagai. I discovered he was one of the special guards, hidden in holes in the grounds, and it was his job to persuade people not to creep about wearing assagais.

Before camping at Earl's Court the following night—at another place with a staircase and jug—I had stopped to examine a map. An old lady appeared at the window of the car and asked me where I lived. I told her *I* didn't even know where I lived, but drove her nevertheless the ten miles to where she thought she should be. She suddenly asked me to stop outside a house in a half-mile terrace of dwellings, thanked me and said she was home at last. She went inside, leaving me to find my camp spot ten miles back. Why did these things always happen to me?

Checking out of the room with the jug early, I made for Madame Tussaud's waxworks to see what the candle-grease people looked like. I had heard visitors often carried on a one-sided conversation with a strategically placed dummy before finding it was made of wax. I determined that this wouldn't happen to me. As I went in I saw one such dummy standing by a stairway, I went over to it feeling that someone was waiting to have a laugh, but instead of talking to it I patted it on the cheek, only to receive an instant reaction as an indignant bona fide usher bellowed "ere, wot's goin' on?' I just couldn't win. Soon I came to an exhibit showing the actual guillotine blade which was used to make Marie-Antoinette so angry that she lost her head completely. Visualising her head lying on the ground made me think of the policeman at Chartwell. I had always thought a guillotine blade as being razor-edged, but this was blunt and angled like in cartoons, with the heavy block of wood joined to the upper edge, giving it enough weight to push it through an average neck. This must have saved a lot of work constantly sharpening the grizzly object. I wondered how the wax model of Ned Kelly would have stood up to the heat in Australia, and hurried off to the Tower of London.

The men marching about and I had only one thing in common: we were bully beef eaters, but there the resemblance ended. I had never worn scarlet bloomers with yellow frills above full-length red stockings, and my hat in the bush did more to keep the sun out of my eyes than theirs did. I thought I'd mistaken The Tower for a circus at first, but was reassured when I went inside to see the dungeons for *the enemy*, things to torture *the enemy*, and pig iron suits to wear so *the enemy* couldn't hurt them back. It was hardly cricket, what ho! They must have sounded, as they rode about on their horses, like our Afghan hawkers selling dishes and frying pans to the cattle station homesteads. Even the horses were dressed to kill. It would have taken most of the day to get ready for the fray, when it would have been time to knock off, to oil their joints before hanging them up for the night.

I then left the car outside a place called New Scotland Yard, almost under the shadow of Big Ben. I took a ride on a river bus to Greenwich to see the observatory. It is at Greenwich, of course, where a line on a brass plate marks the zero meridian of the world, which was where all the longitude observations I had taken in Australia originated. After photographing the line where east longitude changed into west longitude, I called into the National Maritime Museum at the base of Observatory Hill and had the great satisfaction of seeing Lord Nelson's socks. I continued into the room where Harrison's four chronometers were preserved in glass cases. They were his life's work, made two centuries before and were still in perfect working order. He had won the prize offered to the person who could build a precision time-piece for use in world navigation and discovery, thus allowing accurate astronomical observations to be carried out by the ancient mariners. I had been using chronometers in the bush for twenty years and it was quite interesting to see the forerunners of these, keeping time irrespective of changes of temperature. Harrison's prize winner was in a case declaring it was the actual one used by Captain Cook in his discovery of Australia. Walking past the socks, I made an inspection of the wooden anchor hanging on the side of the Cutty Sark. This was the last of the tea clippers and was in dry dock up on blocks. I knew it was a wooden anchor, as the cross-piece at the bottom was dovetailed to the shaft and was also made of wood.

I went over to get the car and noticed it was still the only one parked at that spot: it wasn't a regular parking zone. I got away with it as it must have been just too small a job for Scotland Yard to bother with. The morning after staying at Harry Higgs' place, we went for a drive through Richmond Park. While eating sandwiches in the car I felt a hot breath on my neck. As I spun around I found I was face to face with a reindeer who had put his head right inside the car. He refused to take it out again until I had issued a piece of cake. With that, another came over, much to the delight of the Higgs family who were ready for them. This one was wearing a pair of antlers four feet across, which stopped him from getting his head into the car. Instead, he wedged them against the door and needed cake before he could move. Ordinary sandwiches wouldn't do and I was wondering how I was going to explain away the scratches to the owner of the car. He'd think I was some kind of a nut if I told him a reindeer had attacked me on the trip.

Once again in London, after spending the night drawing *foul fiends* for Rowland, I spent a free period ringing up people from our atom bomb tests in Australia. I had a book—which I only needed a small hydraulic jack to move—called *Who's Who*. A visit to Windsor Castle with some friends from Hatch End followed the next day where I saw a picture of a lady wearing a long silver fur overcoat. I finished up about 3 inches from it to assure myself the fur wasn't real, and asked a guard nearby who had drawn it as I couldn't have done it better myself. He was very polite as he explained it was an original Van Dyke. Outside I stared at several boys wearing silk top hats and white stiff collars four inches high. I asked my friends what was the matter with their necks; apparently they were from Eton. I never did discover what was the matter with them.

The trip to Brighton the next day took us through Pease Pottage. I thought they were kidding until I was told it had something to do with a pudding. I replied carefully 'I see,' which I didn't. The events of the following day were to govern the rest of my stay in England and the route chosen for my ultimate flight back to Australia.

Leaving Hatch End early the next day I drove back to London in the bright sunshine and reached Piccadilly Circus via Baker Street—where Sherlock Holmes camped. I was stopped in my lane of heavy traffic waiting for the lights to change to green. As I sat, a car eased alongside mine and the driver called over to me: 'Excuse me old chap, but your tail light is on and has been for some time.' I called out my thanks, saying it must be the brake light which I would have a go at fixing in the paddock at Bedford Square. With that, he pulled down the sunglasses he'd needed ever since I came to England and excitedly exclaimed he had seen me before, '...at the atom bomb site in Australia.' I brightened up at this although I didn't know him, and yelled out above the honking of the horns that it sounded pretty right. He yelled back 'Look here, follow me through the traffic and we'll sort it out.' To add somewhat to the vexation of the drivers behind, I waited until he had manoeuvred into the lane of cars in front of me after which we moved off.

The stranger stopped next to the small caged-in paddock where I had been headed as a likely parking place, according to the map on the seat beside me. He leapt out, opened my door and began beating me across the shoulder blades, asking what on earth was I doing in England? I managed to gasp out that I was sitting in a car being beaten across the shoulder blades. I thought he could see that for himself, but it soon came out that he was present at the atomic tests in Australia on behalf of the RAF in which he was a Wing Commander. His name completely eluded me. When he found I was homeless, he asked what my intentions were for the next couple of months. He invited me to stay at his home at Sandy Lodge in Northwood. I was to accompany him to Leicester on a business trip on the following day.

I was pleased as fury at this, so left my car at the paddock in the cage, after moving a locked motorbike away from a space ample for the car. From then on I never failed to find a parking spot in London at Bedford Square, even though I had once temporarily attached myself to the council and swept up a heap of leaves higher than the car in the last vacant spot, shovelled them into an enormous waiting barrow, then wheeled them all around the corner.

Travelling with the Wing Commander in his car, we drove to his office near Aldwych where he warned his wife that an Australian bushman was coming home with him. The riddle of his name was solved by the swooning of a receptionist on whose desk he dropped his card. She picked it up and all but passed out during which diversion I studied the card to see James Stewart written across it.

That night, after being shown more of London by my newly-found expert, we drove to Bedford Square where I collected the Vauxhall. I spent the rest of the afternoon trying to follow James through the London maze to Northwood. After tea we had a talk about our old 'bomb days' in Australia. Kay, his wife and son Andrew were pleased to see my slides of Australian aborigines. Andy produced a book and a pencil for some bush sketches. It was a wonderful high-gabled house with two storeys and even had dressing rooms. The whole place was surrounded by a colourful garden and I was shown upstairs to the room where I'd be sleeping, complete with H. and C. I didn't know what the dressing room was for as all I had to put on was the extra shirt.

Early the next sunny morning we were off to Leicester, from where hob-nailed boots originated, along a new road being built to Birmingham. It was a two hundred-mile return trip and my first look at central England.

KAY had made some survey cakes for tea and after another travel talk about my trip over the USA we prepared for a new onslaught on London in the morning. Jimmy had been an RAF pilot in the second world war. He planned my itinerary for an ideal return trip to Australia, very ably helped by Kay. As I lay down I thought of the incredible coincidence which had led to our meeting in the London traffic, after six years and twelve thousand miles from our camp in Central Australia.

I called in to see Ivor Bowen, an extremely pleasant English gentleman who had accompanied Sir William Penney to Australia in preparation for the atomic bomb trials. He was at his office in Throgmorton Street near the London Wall. As I was ushered in to Ivor's office by his secretary, I asked her if she could visualise Mr Bowen sitting in the desert eating a half-cooked goanna. She admitted she couldn't. Ivor, seated behind his great glass-topped desk across an expanse of thick carpet, backed up my story. She padded out wide-eyed to tell the rest of the staff, as Ivor and I burst out laughing.

'It makes a good sunshade.'

Later I felt a trifle out of place in Threadneedle Street, as I rubbed shoulders with men in top hats, striped trousers and carrying umbrellas. I was in my desert boots, belt and hunting knife. At one shop full of the works of Dickens and Shakespeare, I saw a boy of barely twenty studying the dusty volumes through the grimy glass. He was wearing a black bowler hat, a tight black suit with white things hanging down around his black polished shoes. He had a high stiff collar like a length of bore casing, and in his white silky hand he carried a furled umbrella. The sun was beating down and beads of perspiration were rolling from the great mop of sandy hair bulging out from the bowler. I ambled over to him with thumbs hooked into my belt and asked him why he didn't put up his umbrella to use as a sunshade? He turned stiffly to me with a most withering look flashed back to me from over his nose, then returned his attention to the volumes. I would have liked to have had him out on one of my camps in the desert: he was probably a very nice boy.

A visit to Banbury Cross was arranged for Sunday. Jimmy and Kay were to call for their other son, Peter, at boarding school where he was breaking up for the holidays. I'd heard of Banbury Cross since I was three, but now I knew they had been kidding all along as I couldn't see any ladies wearing bells on their toes.

In the London airline office the next day I handed in the itinerary drawn up by Jimmy and Kay for my return to Australia in two months time. While waiting in the office for it all to be finalised, a man strolled past the desk and grabbed my book of tickets. I was set to tackle him when I recognised him. Here, in London, was the very man who had written out my tickets in Adelaide and had been so helpful at the start of my trip back home. He had recognised his own writing on the tickets lying on the desk and I was able to thank him in person for his efficiency.

My eyes were growing sore and red-rimmed from the diesel fumes of London buses. Traffic threw up grime and dust with never-ending consistency. I'm sure the dust had angles on it as it grated away at my eyes, which were quite unused to it. It didn't seem to worry anyone around me. After cutting Peter and Andy's hair that night in Northwood, I prepared to take my leave of the kindest people a lone bushman could meet. I promised to accept their offer to call again when I'd completed my expedition around the UK, which I was to resume in the morning.

Chapter 7

BRITISH HOSPITALITY

'FOR heaven's sake, will you leave that machine-gun alone!
I only want to see Sir William.' The English gentleman
who had been walking his setter pronounced it 'Slough.'
When I asked for directions after leaving Jimmy and Kay, I had
finally driven through 'Slosh.' After that I became engaged in
battle with the uniformed guards of the main gate at the Atomic
Weapons Research Establishment at Aldermaston. I had driven
up, ambled into the guard house and said I'd like to have a yarn
with Sir William Penney, the Director of the establishment. The
guard's cap seemed to fall over his eyes, but it was really his
eyebrows going up to meet it—as he saw the knife on my belt—
causing him to reach under the table where I was sure a sub
machine-gun was hidden. He probably guessed I came from
Australia, but he wasn't to know that Sir William had invited me. I

had been invited to call and see him, and all the friends with whom I had worked with back home, surveying the site for the atom bomb tests. The guard ordered: 'Be off with you.' When I asked 'Off with me what?' he made another grab.

The trouble was caused by the delay at *Slosh* which made me ten minutes late. I had said over the telephone at Castlewood House I would be there at eleven o'clock. The guards had been warned not to shoot, but unfortunately they had been replaced at eleven exactly, so these were a new batch. They were all set to put me under arrest when they realised I didn't want to be *off with me* (as though I could be off *without* me), and commenced making notes during which they asked my name. The effect of this was astounding: one plunged at the phone and saluted into it as he said: 'Sir William! Mr Beadell has just this minute arrove.' Soon afterwards a figure came walking to the guardhouse and I shook hands with one of the most brilliant atomic scientists in the British Empire.

The last time I had seen him was out in the bush at the Maralinga bomb testing range twelve thousand miles away. I had come in from a survey trip, wearing dusty, torn rags, held together with the same belt as I had on this day. The guard, a new man already, appeared behind me with a book and poised pen, coughed discreetly and asked for my particulars to complete his duty. I could personally guarantee it was performed with a remarkable high standard of efficiency as demanded by such a top-secret establishment. He came to the question of nationality when Sir William replied for me with a serious face, 'Abo of course, what did you think?' As the guard studied his book he said: 'Why yes Sir, of course,—er—how do you spell it, Sir?' I was free to drive the Vauxhall through the gate, after he had seen the contents of the other sinister-looking pouch on my belt.

Old Ted Marshall had come ambling along to meet me by then. He was an extremely likeable Englishman to whom I had supplied all my survey information about the bomb range in Australia. He kept it safely for use when needed, and I was pleased to discover that Ted was going to show me around. Sir William had to leave to keep an appointment, but arranged that I stay at his house, after seeing all my friends. He left in his glittering black Jaguar.

Some signs had been placed on various notice boards by Ted, warning of my visit. Everything possible had been done with characteristic English precision to enable me to make the most of my week's stay. I didn't see my car—or other shirt—for the next four days.

Ted proceeded to take me around to see the friends I had made in the bush. They were now back in their offices scattered about within the establishment buildings. The tour included a view inside the official mess, where visitors such as the Duke of Edinburgh were entertained. As I stared about the big room, Ted stood silently alongside me and eventually my eyes strayed to the wall over the top table. There, hanging among the various mementoes of the British atomic trials, was a huge gold frame around a water colour painting of an Australian aboriginal. I had painted it myself and given to Sir William during the Australian tests. Ted laughed—until a spasm of coughing took over—at my surprise on seeing it in such surroundings. I wondered how many of the V.I.P. visitors had nightmares after eating with this wild and carefree bearded native from the bush. I remembered the camp where I had found the subject. The thought cheered me up to a point of being almost homesick.

At the time arranged on the notice boards, Ted had me inside the lunch hall to meet the atomic team. I couldn't help noticing how very neat everyone looked, suddenly realising we had never seen each other without the dust and clouds of flies in the bush. I had a feeling I didn't look much different, being still in my desert boots and knife belt. It was a most pleasant reunion, after which the plan was that I should accompany Ted to stay at his house in Basingstoke for the night. At Aldermaston the following day two documentary films of the Australian trials were screened for me. I was in them, cooking porridge in a billy and stirring with a dry mulga stick. I had been required to drive my Land Rover up to the camera, get out in the heat of the day, in a place where it rains once every year, look up to the sky to see if the sun happened to be shining—and carry out a sun observation to find my position in the bush. I couldn't help smiling when I thought how I'd quickly put a stop to the rain in England as well, but it was good to see the sandhills and mulga again, so very far away.

Dr John Dawson had planned to put up with me at his place in Reading that night. I discovered that he owned two dogs, each about the size of a pony. I asked him where he kept the saddles and bridles, as they stood in front of me with their forepaws on my head, nearly pushing me through the floor. He assured me they were playing when he saw me going for the hunting knife. I only hoped they never got rough with anyone. After tea we all went for a quiet evening drive along the hedge-lined lanes. It would have been very relaxing, if it hadn't been for the eighty miles an hour he was doing, crouched over the wheel, while the dogs and I hugged each other in his open-topped car. The scarf around his neck was cracking like a stockwhip as it flew straight out behind. Mrs Dawson leaned back in the leather seat nonchalantly, pointing out things of interest as they streaked by.

We arrived at an open grassed hill upon which a man was hanging by his neck from a gallows swaying gently in the breeze. As I started thinking that *here* was something you didn't see every day, it occurred to me that he was probably one of John's previous passengers, who had chosen that way out of making the return journey with him. John casually informed me that this was known as a gibbet, generally used to leave highwaymen hanging for all to see, as a deterrent. The birds had soon made the robbers look like someone out of Madame Tussaud's 'Chamber of 'orrers'—as the usher there had told me it was called. I climbed unsteadily up the hill to see this grizzly object, only to find it was a straw man, sewn in hessian and hung there for effect.

After a further inspection of the A.W.R.E., the night was spent at Bill Saxby's bungalow, drawing more bush pictures for his small daughter Sally. They were all wondrous people to me, and I could only show them the slides of bushland in return. Everything had been organised, even a cable sent to our Weapons Research Establishment in South Australia, informing them I was gradually turning the sedate Aldermaston into bedlam.

The next day I sought a car to drive to Heather House, where Sir William lived with his family. Ted had spent some time on the telephone planning visits to several places I wished to see: this included the Land Rover factory in Solihull and the Farnborough Air Show later in the year with George Hicks. George had kindly been arranging that for me. I had met him at the Woomera bombing range nine years before.

LADY Penney opened the door; 'You must be Lennie Beadell. Your shirt looks as though it has been slept in for days, give it to me immediately to clean.' She was so matter-of-fact about everything that I felt at home straight away. She obviously had a sense of humour. When she saw me hesitating, she repeated 'Well, give it to me,' holding out her hand and sounding like an Australian. I must have been the only person to walk into Heather House wearing desert boots, a knife belt and no shirt. She showed me the upstairs room where I would be camping. There was a pair of kangaroo-skin mats I'd shot for Sir William. Later, I went down to the car to fetch my other shirt from the 'Igh 'Ob'n' bag.

Sir William came home in the black Jaguar as we were peeling potatoes for tea. He was handed a knife to get on with the beans as soon as he walked into the kitchen. Lady Penney informed me she was known to her friends as 'Lady P,' and wouldn't have all this atom business interfering with their home. She quickly proved herself to be a most happy and delightful hostess.

The main business of the evening was to pack up the car for a trip the following day. We were to go to their younger son's school break-up and sports day, at Cranleigh, forty miles south-east of Aldermaston. I was getting to see more of the English countryside; it was easy on the eyes after the sandhills and desert. The main trouble experienced at the school was that the hot sun kept on moving. This caused Sir William to wake up repeatedly under the oak tree, where he was sleeping on a copy of The *London Evening News*. He had to do this in order to shift it back into the shade.

Dinner was in the open, with the tablecloth brought by Lady P. straddling a narrow pathway through the bracken in the woods.

Apart from the scenery and the wonderful food, it took on the atmosphere of a survey dinner camp in the bush. Another difference was the people, who would periodically stroll along hand-in-hand (unless they were married), politely bid us 'Good afternoon,' step around the cloth and carry on. I was thinking how a similar scene would have gone in Australia. The strollers would have stamped on your bread, smearing the butter over everything else they put their boots in, knocking over several mugs of tea on the way, and then asking why the squatting galahs couldn't get out of the road.

That night was spent in recounting the hundreds of funny experiences at the atomic camp in Australia. Lady P. and the boys were in tears of laughter. My trip across the USA finished them off completely.

Oxford, to the north, was to be my target the next day. The Penneys planned to visit Sir John Cockroft at Harwell. I had heard there was quite a good school at Oxford. I found the main street looked like an eroded valley with rock walls. Although there was no firewood about, I had dinner in a paddock at the end of town, drinking water out of the billy I carried for the radiator.

There was a boat at Portsmouth everyone insisted I should see. It was called the *Victory* and belonged to the man standing on the post in London, above the pigeons. It was there I drove the day after Oxford. I called into Winchester on the way, my rifle had the same name back in the bush. Driving into the main street, I noticed a sign next to a vacant parking spot, where I left the car and tried to find a table I'd been told about since I was seven years old. I'd know it when I saw it: it was round, like the end of a cable drum used for barbecues. King Arthur spent most of his nights sitting at it. I don't know what he did there, but King Arthur's nights at the round table became quite well-known.

It had a very complicated design on top, but at least it was round, so I shrugged and left the table where it was. I walked back to the car, when I found a uniformed policeman looking after it for me. I unlocked the door and thanked him as he mooched over. He excused himself as he greeted me with a cheery 'Good morning Sir, but I would like a word with you if you don't mind.'

I told him I'd be pleased to, and would he like to take a seat in the car as we chatted. He replied it was kind of me to offer, but had I happened to glance at the notice next to the car? I assured him I had, as it was so helpful. 'Why, I just drove up, saw it, and there was a parking place right away, with no waiting at all, just as the sign said.' The little peak of his hat appeared to lower down over his eyes. He looked up and told me that I was from Australia. I couldn't see how he knew; we had never met before. The conversation went on to include kangaroos and boomerangs, until I mentioned I had better be getting along to see a boat. He saluted as I started the engine, and as I drove away I thought what a thoroughly pleasant man he was.

'It's right too—found this parking spot right off.'

I soon pulled up in Portsmouth, left the car in another friendly *No Waiting* area, and went in search of the *Victory*. It looked like a huge toy, brightly painted and made of wood, but the cannons were real. They were there for *the enemy*. This enemy loomed everywhere I went. I couldn't see what all the trouble had been, as everyone I had met so far was so nice.

Once inside the ship I was struck by how low the roof was. In fact, I was being constantly struck on the forehead just above the eyes. The logs which held up the roof were by no means soft. It took some time to be able to straighten up afterwards. I was getting used to creeping about like the hunchback of Notre Dame. I thought a box I saw was for storing chaff for livestock on long sea trips, but a sailor pointed out that it was Nelson's bed. Although he could never have fallen out of it, even in the roughest of seas, he would have had to watch out for splinters when he turned in for the night. One thing was certain, he could never have been accused of wasting money on his personal comfort.

A polished brass plate screwed to the deck at the top of a flight of stairs was the climax of the inspection of the ship—having been corrected on board after calling it a boat. It marked the exact spot where Nelson was killed. You could picture him being struck down at the height of the sea battle.

A Royal Marine Exhibition was under way as I walked down the planks from the *Victory*. I went over to see the show. A helicopter flew over, to lower a small vehicle to the ground, from which emerged half a dozen soldiers bristling with rifles. The sun shone from their gleaming hob-nailed boots, and after a brief and heated bun fight with *the enemy*, they jumped back into the vehicle and drove off to the ice-cream stand behind some tents. Marquees housed various rockets, nameplates of which showed they were being tested at Woomera, in Australia. They also showed a photograph of the launching site—the very one I had done the first survey of twelve years before.

I was due to return to Heather House in time for tea, so I collected the car from the *No Waiting* area and drove back through Basingstoke like fury. The topic of conversation that night was onions, and how large Sir William could grow them. When I saw his crop, I thought they must have been watermelons. Lady P. took a photograph of us in the middle of the conversation, as I held up an imaginary onion from down under, the size of a weather balloon.

I drove away from Heather House in the morning, following the black Jaguar Sir William drove through the gates, past the machine-guns, into the establishment. Lady Penney had given me a cookery book for use in the bush. So, with my 'Igh 'Ob'n bag and shirt, I headed off to Farnborough to see some friends prior to the air show. This was another place which had guards with itchy trigger fingers, but after a phone call, I was inside without the use of a bullet-proof vest. John Mercer was in his office and I remembered giving him a lift in Adelaide, one rainy night many years ago.

I had heard of people of 'no fixed place of abode' as the police put it. I was certainly one of the club. My arrangement for that night was to find my way to Mortimer, where Frank Hill lived. It was Frank's thumb that had been used to push the red button which triggered off several atomic bombs at Maralinga. I was to stay with him before continuing the expedition. His house was straight out of a picture, only better. It was set to one side of a large expanse of lawn, surrounded by woods, with a rockery of brilliant flowers. Frank and his wife Anne came out, as I was sitting, spellbound, in the car realising that for a quarter of a century I had known there must somewhere be a better place than the jumbled mess of sandhills that were my home. At last I had found it.

Putting my shirt in the allotted room, I walked about the grounds with Frank. We went to his glass hot-house—having added botany to the list of sciences in which he was expert. The glass vent in the roof was actuated by a gear wheel meshed into a semicircular toothed sprocket. This in turn was operated automatically by fluctuations in temperature. When the cold nights came, the vent would gradually shut. If the sun came out the next morning, the vents would ease open to let out the heat. Inside the house, resting on the mantelpiece, was a cartoon I had drawn at the bomb site. It was, as in most houses I visited, still safely in the possession of its owner after all this time. These were the people who had persuaded me to take a spell from the bush and make this trip around the world.

I casually mentioned how pleased I was to have a ticket for the Farnborough air show, in a month or so. I told Frank my ticket was for the Wednesday of that week. I didn't know he was making a note of that for use later.

ON the move once again the next morning, after a most pleasant evening, I headed off to Salisbury to see Stonehenge, a structure I'd been waiting to inspect all my life. During the break-up ceremonies at Banbury Cross, I had met a family from Salisbury. They had also been to collect their son for the holiday break. They were the Thesigers who, on hearing of my intentions to visit Stonehenge, immediately insisted that I stay with them while at Salisbury. I asked them what all the brick domes were, growing up out of the paddocks, only to be told they were chimneys. Asking where the fires were, they replied that the smoke came from locomotives. There were no rails to be seen. I wondered as a newcomer whether or not I was being tricked, until I discovered that the trains went under the ground in tunnels. The chimneys were dotted about the paddocks above the line to let out the soot. It was to the Thesiger's house that I was heading on the morning I took leave of Frank and Anne.

Their house in Salisbury had three storeys, with a curved driveway up to the front door. I drove the Vauxhall, crunching on the gravel surface. The boys—Peter and Richard—whom I had also met, remembered me and took me up to see their mother, who was in the middle of an attack of mumps. She waived away my doubts as to whether or not I should trouble them and I was shown to my room on the third floor. I hung my shirt in its usual solitary confinement in the solid oak cupboard.

After lunch Mrs Thesiger was delighted the boys were going to accompany me to Stonehenge. The boys knew the way blindfolded. Soon, I was standing among the three or four thousand year-old monument, just two months to the day since leaving Adelaide.

The first thing I learned was that my old school teacher 'Daddy Longlegs' Roberts didn't know what he was talking about, when he taught us that the Druids had put up Stonhenge for their rituals in the moonlight.

Five different sorts of rock had been used in the construction, some originating from Pembrokeshire, the south-western corner of Wales. For once the structure didn't seem to have anything to do with *the enemy*. Why the workmen didn't build it next door to their quarry is a mystery. Nobody knows why they dragged the stones for two hundred miles before putting them up here. By the size of the rocks, I was certain they would have supplied free dinosaur meat to anyone for the use of a bulldozer. I wondered if they staged an occasional strike for better conditions, as they undoubtedly would now. Someone told me a lintel was found buried on the way, and I was thinking how the foreman would have sacked the careless worker on the spot—much to the latter's delight—even though he would have missed out on the extra time for Saturday work.

If an interested spectator happened to ask what they were doing, I could see them answering that they were dragging twenty-foot rocks from Pembroke to Salisbury—what else?

With many unanswered questions in my mind, such as how they camped on the job, what they ate, what they wore so many thousand years ago, I had to leave this masterpiece, knowing it had been worth every effort I had made to see it. I added my couple of photographs to the countless which were taken, and headed north with the boys who were half asleep with boredom, to view a similar line of rocks pointing almost exactly at Stonehenge, thirty odd miles away. If the ancients could do these things with nothing, I wondered what they could have achieved with theodolites.

On the way to the other line of rocks at Avebury, Peter Thesiger suddenly said in a very English voice, as he spread the map on his eleven year-old lap, 'Look here, I say old boy. We are on the wrong road, I fear.'

On our return, he pointed out a patch of scrub which was called the New Forest. When we rounded a bend in the road, a small clearing appeared with a rock in it. This, he said, was known as *The Rufus Stone*, where William the Conquerer's son fell over one day. Boys fall over many times a day, so I wasn't sure what was so different about this time.

Back at Salisbury, I enthused with Mr Thesiger about Stonehenge. I talked about it all through tea and into the night, until I climbed the three storeys to my bed. I noticed there was H. and C. laid on to a basin, so I went over to wash off all the Neolithic germs before turning in. I was feeling tired at the thought of all those stones being dragged about by the ancients. When there was enough water in the basin, I turned the tap off— only to see the water gushing faster than ever. The water was almost overflowing. Pulling the plug quickly, I soon realised the hole in the bottom of the sink was incapable of handling the intake. The basin was soon full to overflowing. So, feeling like the boy in Holland, I jammed my thumb into the tap to steady the flow while the thing emptied. This squirted a stream all over me, until I won against the pressure. My thumb started to lose feeling in the freezing water, so I withdrew it. Out poured the water, until I changed thumbs and repeated the operation. I was gradually becoming soaked through my thin shirt. I had visions of the water cascading down the stairs if I let go for more than a few seconds. I tried to think of a way out without calling for someone to relieve me, as it was quite late by this time. I considered grabbing my shirt and ramming it into the tap, with the handle of the hunting knife, but there wasn't time between thumb changes. I decided to make a try for the chair, as this looked like being rather a session, but the only one available was in the far corner of the room. The stairs would have taken on the appearance of Niagara Falls by the time I fetched it.

At that moment Mr Thesiger appeared at the door and started laughing at my predicament, until the tears rolled down his face, making him almost as wet as I was. In between fits of laughter he informed me he had anticipated this happening, as it always does, and he had come up to simply turn off a third tap underneath the basin. This he did, stopping everything immediately. He ambled off down the stairs, still laughing, and said he ought to have it fixed, in case a future visitor didn't have a large enough thumb. I wrung out three gallons of water from my shirt and hung it over the radiator to dry

The next day I found my thumbs had thawed-out and I accompanied Mr Thesiger to Salisbury Cathedral, after thanking everyone for their kindness and help, especially with the plumbing arrangements.

Outside the famous cathedral he tried to drive away to work, but couldn't get his car to start. After working on the bent choke cable I felt I had repaid him a little for the previous evening. I farewelled him there, and inspected the wonderful building. With the most vivid recollections of the many experiences I'd had concerning British hospitality, I headed straight for Dartmoor.

Chapter 8

THE MAIN EXPEDITION

I T was a pity that such wide open, weather-beaten, wind-swept undulations were known to most people because of a compulsory boarding house. Dartmoor was the only place I really felt at home in England. It gave me the feeling of freedom I had been used to away from everything, including the London traffic, which kicked up its angle dust. London's exhaust pipes, pouring out diesel fumes, added to the rawness of already red-rimmed and smarting eyes.

Driving through the moors I could see why so many stories had been written about escaped convicts dragging themselves over the wilds, one jump ahead of the police bloodhounds, waist-deep in mud. It was a wonder that some didn't leap bareback onto the brumbies roaming about and charge off across the plains as Ned Kelly would have done.

My reason for travelling to Tavistock was that, for two decades, I had used a theodolite on surveys in the desert which had been named after the town. Apparently a conference was held to design the instrument in Tavistock. I also wanted to enjoy the feeling of being at home on Dartmoor for as long as possible. In Tavistock I picked up the first of a long list of hitchhikers, a German named Oalf, who stayed put in the car until nightfall to guard against any likelihood of my driving off without him. We had a dinner camp at a little cottage with a built-in café. A girl with a constantly alarmed expression, who had never been further than a mile from the house, served us. Oalf had me pay his bill, as he suddenly found enough English words to explain that he was a bit short. We hurried on to Land's End. At Marazion I saw a little rocky island to the south with a castle on top which, according to the map, was called St. Michael's Mount. As the water was too shallow for ships and looked too deep for hiking, I wondered how St. Michael came in for provisions. He probably built it to keep away from *the enemy*, or it could have been to escape from the mosquitoes.

As we passed through Penzance I kept a lookout for all those pirates I'd heard about, but they must have been cleared out and moved to Dartmoor. With ten miles left to go to get to the south-western tip of England, I had the feeling the road was becoming narrower by the minute. The fence posts were almost touching the car. When we arrived the road suddenly swelled out into a blob at the end. As this was the only place where you could leave your car without obstructing following traffic, I drew over to one side. Before I had a chance to switch off, a weedy little man was at my window demanding the few pence parking fee. I resolved to carry a pair of wire cutters with me next time I visited Land's End. I thought of the reception the little man with the bag would have received if he had approached someone parking in a paddock in Australia.

Oalf went off exploring on his own, with one eye on the scenery and the other glued to the car. As I reached a cliff edge a girl came rushing over to ask me if I could help her. I readied myself for some calamity. Instead, she told me that her boyfriend had a camera and when I replied that was nice for him, she explained that it wouldn't work on its own. After agreeing with me that not many did, she led me over to where he was standing on a rock. She pointed out that they wanted to have a photograph of themselves arm-in-arm, and this would be feasible if I were to take the picture with their machine. At the close of this operation they insisted on using my camera to return the favour. As nothing would satisfy them until they had, I stood on the rock and glanced around behind me, only to see several-hundred feet straight down to the sea bashing against the base. As well as being Land's End it was very nearly Beadell's End, I thought, as I regained possession of the instrument. Ambling back to the car I found Oalf already clutching the door handle.

It was almost camping time after we headed off on the coast road towards Devon. I began to wonder what I was going to do with jolly old Oalf. All along the road were farmhouses displaying 'Bed and Breakfast' signs. Stopping, the landlady apologised for having room for only one guest. I magnanimously told Oalf that I'd be only too pleased to let him have it while I struggled on to find another for myself, allowing him to resume his hitchhiking in the morning. I was so relieved to hear his grateful acceptance as I didn't look forward to paying his bills indefinitely. I drove off perhaps a little too rapidly.

At St. Ives, a little further on, another sign prompted me to slide my hunting knife to the rear of my belt as I went in. A very jolly Cornish lady came to the door of the farmhouse to tell me where to leave the car: by the cow yard where her husband was almost through with the milking. Her two children aged nine and ten rode with me, after which we all went inside to sit in the warm kitchen. As I'd left the shirt in the 'Igh 'Ob'n bag outside, I had nothing to put in the room allotted, so we just started right in to talk about Australia. Paper and pencils were produced and I spent the time drawing pictures of the bush for the interested children already sitting on my lap and shoulders. Seven pages of sketches later, farmer Giles clomped into the kitchen with a bucket of milk in each hand and two blobs of mud for feet; which were revealed upon removal of his clod hoppers.

I shook his hand, covered in dried milk, and we all sat down to Cornish tea in the warmth of the kitchen.

As they were clearing away, having refused to let me help, I told the boy he could do with a survey trim and went out to the car for my hair clippers, which I carried to cut my own. Shortly afterwards the kitchen floor was covered in matted hair from the children. The farmer and I then sat on the floor for a demonstration of how I cut my own hair in the Australian bush, using two mirrors. By the time I had tied myself into the necessary knots, the usually quiet kitchen had turned into bedlam with the old farmer slapping his knees in hysteria as his wife mopped tears off her face with a tea towel. It was midnight by the time the children's bags were full of bush sketches and we all went off to bed.

Five minutes later I heard the rattle of the milk buckets and struggled out to see the clod hoppers disappear into the cow yard. It was really 4.30a.m. After porridge—floating on a plate of cream—and fresh eggs with home-baked bread, I reluctantly decided it was time to head off again. The family gathered around the car to say goodbye. The bed and breakfast had cost a mere fifteen shillings compared to the fifteen dollars at *Pennsylvania 6-5000*. I knew where I enjoyed staying the most.

SURVEYOR John Richmond, my old friend in Sydney, had been kind enough to accommodate Monica Boulter, a nurse from Bristol, on her working holiday in Australia. I had been told to be sure and call in to see her family. It didn't look to be too far—by Australian standards—from where I was, near Land's End, so Bristol was to be my goal for that night. Jimmy Stewart had advised against the coast road south of the Bristol Channel, being steep and very winding, but that was the way I chose. Or rather two German girl hitchhikers chose it for me, as they wanted to stay at a resort on the way. By the time I had reached Somerset I could see what Jimmy had meant, but it was worth it. The journey included many miles of the beautiful Devon countryside. To view it meant first removing my desert boots in order to climb on the roof of the Vauxhall, to see over the high hedges.

Calling into Wells, I thought I should also include the town of Bath on the way. As I got to the baths in Bath the great doors were just being closed, preventing me from going in to see where the Romans washed themselves after fighting with *the enemy*. I visualised a large tub where they all jumped in together after taking off their iron clothes, but I was informed it was more complicated than that. They even had underground heating and lead pipes. It being late afternoon, I drove on the dozen miles to Bristol; I soon found Richmond Hill. I knocked on the solid door of Number 20.

THE door opened and a lady stood there with a puzzled expression. I explained that I was Len—but that was as far as I got. She told me the rest about myself, saying she had been sent a newspaper article from my surveyor friend John in Australia and she recognised me from the picture. She told me her husband was a dentist and was at his surgery in the house. Monica would be home after hospital hours. Another girl came in and was introduced as Christine, their other daughter, who was a doctor. After a while, one of the happiest-looking men I had ever seen, came in wearing a snow-white coat with hair to match, and shook hands. He was on the wrong side of normal retiring age, but still as fit as he had ever been. He had read the newspaper story which included a description of my bush dentistry, with the refinement of injections. This resulted in him naming me on the spot: *Lennie the Lancer*. Monica arrived not long after that. I had last see her at John's place in Sydney, and we all had quite a lively talk. They were all astounded to hear I'd just come in from Land's End. I was given a room, into which I placed the shirt from the car. Later we all drove around Bristol in the Vauxhall with Doctor Boulter navigating. The suspension bridge over the gorge was on the list of places to see. The story was re-told of how, donkeys years ago, a lady had done her best to commit suicide by jumping off the bridge into the ravine. She had forgotten to take off her crinoline first. This had parachuted her down safely. Apart from it feeling a bit drafty on the way down, she was unharmed.

The next day Christine volunteered to show me the rest of Bristol in the daylight, which included a visit to the hospital where

I sat sipping coffee among a group of nurses. Not being used to such a bevy of girls I was beginning to feel a little uneasy. Soon we were on the way to see where the Bristol freighters, which had often supplied me out in the bush, were made. One shed looked about the size of a sheep station; Christine explained it was where the Brabazon was made.

That night we once again had a slide show of Australia. I was glad I had brought them along.

The next day being Sunday, we all went off to see the Roman bathtubs which I had missed. Compared to my occasional shower—with a bucket full of holes—in the bush, it was apparent they had taken more trouble. On to Wells again where a castle kept off *the enemy*. We had some scones in a place where I again beat my head on the wooden beams holding up the ceiling. England must have been inhabited by pygmies.

We were due to attend a church service on the way back to Bristol. We hurried off, stopping just once to see a vertical crack in an otherwise smooth cliff face where the man who had written *Rock of Ages* was sheltering from a storm at the time. Everything was full of interest, as long as there was someone to point things out.

The church, built in 1300, was half-way up a steep grassy hill. The congregation, before our arrival, had numbered two, not including the minister himself. We swelled it to seven and, after the service, the minister asked me to sign their visitors' book. There was a column for addresses and I was at rather a loss as to which mulga tree I lived under, so simply put Woomera Rocket Range. He showed me the details of the church, including a lepers' enclosure where the unfortunate people were required to sit apart from the congregation. They had to peep at the pulpit through small slots in the thick rock wall.

I said a reluctant goodbye to the Boulters next morning. I was off again north to Gloucester and Tewkesbury where, as a result of the phone calls at Castlewood House, I was due to drop in to see General Sir John Evetts. Sir John was in charge of the small group of half a dozen men from the UK touring the world in 1946 in search of a likely place to develop a rocket range. Their search had brought them to Australia and later plane flights indicated areas to the north-west of Port Augusta to be suitable. This area consisted of millions of square miles of almost completely uninhabited and unexplored land, stretching to the Indian Ocean. I had met him in his hotel in Adelaide in 1947, twelve years before. I had been selected to locate details and carry out a full-scale survey of this area.

There was a Major Wynn-Williams with the party, who always had much paperwork to do relating to the new project. It was he who had named the site Woomera. He obtained this word from an Aboriginal-English dictionary: the word *launcher* had leapt at him from the page. He learned that the aborigines launched spears with a *woomera* and decided it would be an appropriate name for a place to launch rockets. From then on in his reports he referred to the site as Woomera.

General Evetts had called into our survey camp periodically. First he worked with Lindsay Lockwood from the army survey corps, and later Walter Relf, another surveyor from the army.

NOW here I was in the UK on my way on this day to visit the General. Would he remember me so far removed in time and place? Although still in desert boots and watch belt with hunting knife, I had replaced my usual uniform of rags with complete clothes. In turn I wondered if I would remember him. He had often worn long shorts to his knees, with long socks drawn up to within an inch of them, allowing space for the breeze. The shorts were made of vertically-ribbed dark green velvet which contrasted sharply with his snowy knees. These were seen momentarily as the eighteen-inch diameter of the shorts flapped. He was a wonderful person, and had fitted well into our camp during his brief visits. He was, in fact, a truly English gentleman General. The address to which I was now on my way was his latest, which I had read in *Who's Who*. At Kemerton, near Tewkesbury, I asked a man sweeping leaves from his front gate if he knew where General Evetts lived. Everyone hereabouts knew where Sir John's house was and I was told to drive to a large pair of gates leading into a gravel driveway. I drove straight in on the crunching gravel. I was about to switch off the engine outside a beautiful old English house when a man in velvet trousers rushed over, slapped me on the shoulder and exclaimed 'Well, bless my soul! If it isn't Lennie Beadell.' I was amazed at his memory, for which he was already noted, and he went on 'Upon my word!' As I commented on his remembering me he said—'As if anyone could forget.' I wasn't quite sure how to take this, as he still hadn't seen the hunting knife. After climbing out of the car he asked me what I was doing in England. I thought it was obvious, but nevertheless I replied that I was standing there talking to him.

We went over to a rustic table and chairs where a small group was sitting having a tea party and I was introduced to Lady Evetts, Colonel and Mrs Evetts, and a small boy playing nearby at a stream trickling through the grass-covered yard. Colonel Evetts, his son, was from 'Redford Barracks in Edinburgh, ay what!'. On learning that I was on a car trip around the UK he immediately invited me to call into the barracks the moment I arrived in Edinburgh, to meet the members of the mess. He was the current C.O. of that establishment.

It was then his small son was called over to meet *The Australian*. His manners were perfect. After enquiring about the health of the kangaroos he asked: 'I say, Sir, but what is it like down under?' I asked him 'Down under what?' It wasn't too long before he had produced a book and pencil and we spent a while illustrating my answers with sketches. He was engrossed by this, as were Lady Evetts and the Colonel, who asked detailed questions on subjects such as the aerodynamics of boomerangs.

We had an aerodrome at Woomera, used for the pilotless aircraft trials. This was named Evetts Field after the General, so I told the boy that we had an important airfield in Australia named after his grandfather. The General was proud and obviously very attached to his grandson. He beamed as the boy looked up adoringly at him at this news.

They showed me through their two storey house, with the ceiling supports hewn from oak. After three more bruises on my head from the beams, we were back at the tea party. Later, there was an offer of an official pass into the Farnborough Air Show. I was told by the General to be sure and see him at his stall there. He would be selling aeroplane propellers.

It was time to be on my way to the small Rocket Range at Aberporth, near Cardigan, on the west coast of Wales. I had been invited there again as a result of the Castlewood House phone calls. The Evetts gathered around the car as I started the engine. I would see some of them again at Redford and Farnborough.

THAT night, at a bed and breakfast house at Treecastle, I had the use of the bathroom for two hours. The bath lasted two minutes and the rest of the time was used in trying to get out of the door, which had clicked shut in such a way as to make it not respond to the key. I worked on the lock for quite a while with the hunting knife and toothbrush handle, cut to fit and ground to a hook-shape on the window sill. Still the knob would just freewheel. Just as I was preparing to camp on the floor for the night, using the mat as a blanket, I noticed a moveable leg on the bathtub. I used this to make a stronger screwdriver than the knife. I dismantled the whole thing to let the door open. Screwing it all back into place again, and re-installing the iron leg on the tub, I turned in, hoping the next person to use the bath was a blacksmith.

Mid-morning saw the Vauxhall at Aberporth, not far north of where they obtained the rock for Stonehenge. I made for the

Rocket Range Headquarters. To my surprise, the chief superintendent there was Ron Buller, an ex-Woomera man who I knew very well in Australia and soon found most of the staff and I were also well-known to each other. A very comprehensive inspection of the range followed, terminating with lunch and staying the night with Di Reese. He was also a former rip-roaring Woomera man who, since he had married and acquired a young family, had quietened down considerably. After looking over a thing which could never have been built at Woomera—a floating launcher in the sea—Di and his family all climbed into my car and we proceeded on a detailed tour of inspection of the surrounding coastline of Cardigan Bay. This included Cilgerran Castle, built 700 years ago to keep out *the enemy,* with slots and all. William Marshall and Son had a contract to build round-towered castles for anyone who wanted to protect themselves. The son had put up Cilgerran. Old William himself built Pembroke Castle. You could order any sort of castle as long as the tower was round. The tops of the towers were round, as were the tops of the window seats, but these would have been unsafe to sit in because of all the arrows from *the enemy.* It would have been O.K. on the third floor, as the height was out of accurate range. The backs of the fireplaces were also round. It occurred to me Marshall's Castle Construction Company would have been in big trouble if their draughtsman had lost his compass. They must have gone out of business a hundred years later, because an addition here had a pointed top to a doorway. The castle cook would have been the safest as his kitchen was in a place impossible for *the enemy* to touch, except with the use of a helicopter. It showed how all that battling made them appreciate their meals. They must have rushed out for provisions during lulls in the fighting.

The last things to see before going home were the coracles. These were boats made of skin, used for fishing on this part of the Welsh coast. They didn't look as if they would hold more than a dozen sardines, but the design hadn't changed for hundreds of years, so they must have worked. I decided before travelling in one to first remove my watch from its pouch.

Once again I headed off in the morning, this time for Caernarvon, to locate Major Wynn-Williams. I drove through Harlech, where they had a castle built for *the enemy*. I was beginning to think *the enemy* had had the best deal, sitting about watching all these castles feverishly going up for their benefit. They could have sniped at the contractors as they worked over the years the castles took to build, thus sabotaging the effort, instead of waiting to be picked off themselves through the slots.

On the way to Mount Snowdon I found I was singing *Men of Harlech* at the top of my voice, as I drove until I stopped to give two French girl hitchhikers a lift. All I can say about them is that I was glad there were two. They continued north from Betws-y-coed while I carried on west through Pen-y-Gwryd to Cwm-y-glo and then to Caernarvon. I don't know what these were as I couldn't even pronounce them, but at least they all had something in common. I passed by Snowdon on the way, the highest mountain in Wales, at 3,560 feet above mean coracle level. As usual there was only one small area left by the fences in which to park—with the usual fee of sixpence—so I carried right on. I would have liked to have hiked to the top without the normal load of theodolite and tripod, which I was used to, but satisfied myself by continuing on with *Men of Harlech*. I liked the part which went:

March up Snowdon,
With your woad on,
Never mind if you get blowed on—Snowdon,

I was glad I was not having to compete against the French girls *Marseillaise*.

A dozen or so miles further on put the Vauxhall into the township of Caernarvon where the first thing I saw was a castle to keep *the enemy* away. That was before I spotted the ghosts.

Chapter 9

A LULL IN THE TEMPO

THE white apparitions creeping along the main street made Caernarvon look haunted. It didn't appear to be a thing you see everyday, as I had never had the same experience in Australia. The lines of sheets slowly swayed as they progressed at a snail's pace. Becoming concerned, I asked a bystander what was happening, thinking somebody had perhaps opened a dungeon in the castle by mistake. He whispered something about a *bedstead* but still I couldn't see the remotest connection, apart from the sheets.

Wynn-Williams lived somewhere south of the town, so I hurried away with many glances through the rear vision mirror. Soon I had covered the few miles to the address given to me by General Sir John. Shakily climbing out of the car, still with a prickling sensation on my neck, I couldn't help but see through the large windows the back of a man's head, as he sat reading a paper in the front room. I recognised immediately, even after 12 years, Major Wynn-Williams; the man who had named Woomera. His thinning white hair, combed back over the otherwise bald head, with the ends of a white moustache just visible, proved it. I tapped with the heavy door knocker to rouse him. He remembered me straight away and there followed a long session of yarns about our early Woomera days, outside on his lawn. I was able to tell him what Woomera had grown into by now. I told him I had seen the marching apparitions in Caernarvon, with the bystander whispering about the bedstead. I asked him what it was all about. He explained, after he stopped his explosive chuckling, that they were in the middle of a festival known as an Eisteddfod. There was something weird about the sheets, which I didn't dare ask even old Wynn about. He was expecting some visiting relations to stay and directed me to the Prince of Wales Hotel in town to camp for the night. I was to return in the morning for an inspection of a hole which had been left to him in his father's will.

A hole seemed an out of the ordinary sort of thing to leave someone in a will. I was curious to see what it looked like. It actually turned out to be an enormous slate quarry, which was where he had been brought up since boyhood. He showed me the details of the whole business. Slate quarries are as much a part of North Wales as bananas are typical of Queensland. The great lumps of slate from the quarry were carried to a cutting shed, split with a chisel resembling a battle axe, and trimmed with a slowly rotating drum like the blades of a lawnmower. No machine had ever replaced the battle axe and hammer for separating the layers, which parted easily like the leaves of a book. I made a small pile of roof slates in this section myself. In the time I took to make half a dozen an old Welshman next to me had a heap two feet high, but he had been at it since he ran away from home at the turn of the century. The particular day I spent there was rather historic in a way, as the whole works were being converted from steam boilers to electrical power, supplied by diesel generators.

We carried on to circumnavigate Snowdon, via Pont Aber Glaslyn and Beddgelert. We continued to Pen-Y-Gwryd. A more perfectly pleasant countryside I had never before seen. Snow-white sheep were grazing on bright green feed. They watered at the little crystal-clear ponds in the undulations, always with a background view of Mount Snowdon. I thought about that area many times after returning to the dusty hot desert where I worked in Australia.

Tea with the Wynn-Williams, followed by another night at the Prince of Wales Hotel, saw the end of that part of the trip. I drove on to see the small settlement with the longest name in the world. On Wynn's directions I crossed over the Menai Bridge, which joins Anglesey to the rest of Wales. A few miles over the bridge, I saw a railway station with the name plate on a sign. It looked more like the tape feeding out of a news machine. It went on and on until the sign overshadowed the platform for size. I hiked to the other end to see how the story finished. The next step was, of course, to try and say the word which to me was just a jumble of letters, however much I tried. I couldn't even pronounce the recognised abbreviation of Llanfair P.G., because the two L's to begin with had to be said by a Welshman—or an Australian with a mouthful of glue. It had 58 letters on a red sign—with five posts to support it:

LLANFAIRPWLLGWYNGYLLGOGERYCHWYRNDROBW-
LL-LLANTYSILIOGOGOGOCH

A placard showed the translation:

LLAN	FAIR	PWLL	GWYN
church	*Mary*	*a hollow*	*white*
GYLL	GOGER	Y	CHWYRN
hazel	*near to*	*the*	*rapid*
DROBWLL	LLAN	TYSILIO	GOGO GOCH
whirlpool	*church*	*saint's*	*cave* *red*

DRIVING slowly back across the Menai Bridge, still a little stunned, I headed for Liverpool. I passed through Llanfairfechan, a *small*-named place, with the Irish Sea to the north. Not very long after that the road went down into a hole, which led under a creek near Liverpool. It was called the Mersey Tunnel, after the creek, and was three miles long.

I carried straight on north to Preston and camped at a hotel near Lancaster. The way things were going I thought I would probably be sleeping in the car.

One of the most beautiful areas in England was to be seen the next day between this camp and Carlisle. All the main billabongs in England were in a group, with the road threading through them. I would have often liked to have seen the same sight in our own desert, but realised it would not then be a desert anyway. A London girl, Margaret Pink, with her hitchhiking girl colleague, asked for a lift through this district. I was once again more than relieved by the fact there were two of them, because the settlement we inspected immediately afterwards was Gretna Green. The clean white building was signposted as being the first house in Scotland, followed by a description of its main business, namely:

Over 10,000 marriages performed in this marriage room
Est. 1830.

A little further was a blacksmith shop on a rise, with a black painted anvil with *smithy* in white lettering.

The smithy probably made the ring on the same anvil for a little extra cost. A lone piper was playing outside to complete the atmosphere. Margaret and her friend asked me to use their camera on both of them standing at this anvil. I was becoming more nervous by the minute in this place, and was pleased when we finally drove away from Gretna Green. We drove on into Scotland, where the girls went in another direction at Langholm. A phone call had been made from Aberporth to the R.A.F. base at West Freugh. It was connected with the rocket range and I was due to call in that day as a result. This was also near Stranraer, which I had chosen as my hopping off place to make the boat trip to Ireland across the North Sea. It was only about thirty miles away. I had heard the crossing usually made the boats 'stand on end' in the rough Irish Sea. I picked the shortest distance I could find on the map for the crossing as I wasn't a wonderful sailor.

With the dangers of Gretna Green behind me, I soon found West Freugh. I arrived via Maxwelltown where, according to the song, the braes are bonny. I didn't know what braes were at this stage, but I was sure whatever they were they must have been bonny.

West Freugh was a station with guards surrounding it, but as they were expecting me I had no trouble getting in. I met the man belonging to the name I'd been given: Mr Sturgess, a round and very jolly man. In no time I was sitting at a table in the mess room with a banquet in front of me. There followed a question and answer period between the staff and myself, during which they heard tales about Woomera. The rest of the night was spent in a warm bed, which was very welcome.

Leaving the Vauxhall in the middle of the largest garage possible—an empty hanger—the station car drove me to the boat at Stranraer, in the afternoon of the following day. I bought a return ticket to Larne for 37/6. I made myself ready for the rough Irish Sea crossing, but as it turned out, an Irish sixpence could have balanced on its edge on the deck all the way. In keeping with the unusual English weather this was the smoothest crossing ever known to the crew. It seems always the case in these situations, as I discovered once when I took a new mechanic out with me to my camp in the desert. I told him it never rained, but in his first four days with us it didn't stop pouring in this 'arid' country, as he kept calling it, providing him with endless work extracting vehicles bogged up to their windows.

On the way over, a Texan with his daughter and I were having tea at the same table, when the steward asked him for his order. The Texan replied that he was a crazy Yankee and wanted 'a mess of burnt bacon.' They had planned to circumnavigate Ireland counter-clockwise, while I had decided on going the other way. At Larne I walked to a train line and followed it to a platform. I'd already heard Belfast was the main starting place for such a trip. It was dark as I trudged along the streets of Belfast, not knowing where I would be camping for the night. I saw a policeman, who I asked to help me find a place. He looked suspiciously at my hunting knife and asked me where I was going, northern or southern Ireland? He directed me to the Grand Central Hotel in downtown Belfast, where I soon had not only a room, but a hire car to be delivered in the morning.

Walking into the dining room in the morning, I found to my surprise the 'crazy Yankee' and his daughter already there. I joined them once again to listen to the crunching sound of burnt bacon. Not that it couldn't be heard anywhere else in the room.

A wild Irish driver led me out to the Ford Prefect he had waiting. I filled in a form after which he drove me into the stream of traffic, pointing the car in the rough direction of Dublin. At a temporary stop in the flow of traffic, he leaped out, slamming the door and yelled—as he disappeared on foot—that it was all mine. I had to climb over to the seat behind the wheel and hoped it was first gear I had it in as I took off with the moving traffic. As I was at least going forward, I left it in that one gear until clear of the main stream. This vehicle was quite new to me.

In Dublin I stopped to send some cards to Australia, to Jimmy Stewart, and to Bristol from *Lennie the Lancer*. On the way I did notice that the Mountains of Mourn really did sweep down to the sea.

South of Dublin, towards Waterford, hurrying a little too much for this lazy day, I stopped to pick up two Irish boys hitchhiking. As there didn't seem to be any speed limits I carried on quite rapidly. I had made an arrangement to meet the owner in Stranraer in four days' time, so this kept me on the go. I mentioned to the hitchhikers that someone had passed me earlier on. They called out above the noise of the wind whistling past, 'Sure, and he must have been going the other way.' When I had satisfied them he had been heading the same way as I was, they finished the conversation flatly with: 'Then he must have been in an aeroplane with a leprechaun after him.'

Driving via Tipperary, we were soon in Cork where the boys directed me to the youth hostel. I went off to seek a bed which I eventually found in the Victoria Hotel. I promised to call for them again in the morning. Mooching around Cork, I got into a conversation with a policeman, who informed me I was either a Canadian or a New Zealander. He was really delighted by the fact that I was Australian, and told me enthusiastically that he'd just read a story about Australia in a newspaper. He said the article described some surveyors who were pushing new roads into the unexplored desert. I asked him if the name *Gunbarrel Highway* meant anything to him and he literally jumped up and down with excitement as he said 'Sure, and that was the name in the paper.' When I told him that was my camp he tried to run me in, indignantly asking with his quick Irish temper just what I took him for. I could see it was hopeless to explain, so I asked about Cork landmarks. There was an O'Toole store, Hannigan's Butcher's Shop, Patrick Street and O'Reilly the Barber. I remarked to the policeman that they were all certainly good old South African names. He nearly burst a blood vessel. He went quiet, and in a restrained and hushed voice corrected me: 'They're *Oirish*.' I didn't seem to be getting any further with him now that he had a paddy on, so I went to the Victoria Hotel to sleep.

It was uncanny the way that Blarney Stone worked. The two boys I called for warned me if I kissed it, then I'd be married within the year, which later proved to be inaccurate. It took me a year and a half.

We stopped at the foot of the rise Blarney Castle was built on against *the enemy* and walked on up. On the top of the battlements I saw it—a large rock set into the wall—smeared with lipstick and face cream. The famous Blarney Stone. There was a well-worn blanket next to it on which to lie, while a man was employed full time, holding people's knees down as they bent over backwards to add their layer of lipstick to the surface of the rock. There was a man photographing the operation next to a sign which read *Kissing the Blarney Stone*. Each visitor was handed a card to send for the print. The postcard cost you half-a-crown at a place near Plunkett Street in Cork. The ticket was appropriately coloured green.

The hitchhikers pushed me forward and although the attendant didn't give me as much attention as he did the ladies, he nevertheless held me as I kissed the first rock that I had ever kissed in my life. When I came away with the previous ladies' lipstick smeared over my face, it reminded me of the joke where the girl ordered her friend to wipe her silly grin off his face.

They used to have the surface of the stone facing *outside* the battlements, and the victims were held by the ankles as they dangled down. A man at the bottom used to make his living by collecting the watches and pens which fell out of pockets. He sold them to the people as they came out. They made it safer since one attendant let one unfortunate person slip through his fingers, to fall head-first into the ground, where he stuck like a dart. Now they have added an iron grille under the stone, which still allows watches and pens to fall through.

We carried on to Killarney, where the boys left me. As I drove up towards Tralee, I made a wish that I would re-visit this beautiful country at a later date. No wonder the colour green was synonymous with Ireland. At Tralee I stopped for two Irish girls, hitchhiking to Limerick. Their places were taken almost immediately by two Irish women in their 90s on their way to Galway. Limerick was an exceptionally pleasant-looking town which I remembered later, as I read the story of how a large fire had later swept through it. The old ladies, with their enormous sacks, proved to be the most grateful people I had carried. As they struggled over to a small white cottage with a thatched roof, I heard them calling 'and may the good Lord bless you and we'll pray for you night and day and night and day and...' which was still going long after the words had grown too faint to hear.

Driving between rock fences, between paddocks, I finally stopped at Sligo. I passed through Castlebar, where I had got out to wait for a procession of pigs and chooks ambling down the main street. I saw a group of old men staring at me, watching my every move. When I had shut the door I turned to see them all leaning over to check up on just what I was doing. Glancing over to the other side of the street, several more were craning their necks over the pigs to study my moves and soon I found I was under the close scrutiny of everyone within range. I felt as if in possession of two heads. By then the chooks had divided, and the pigs were grunting slowly away, so I climbed back into the car and carefully drove off through this mobile zoo. In the rear vision mirror I saw them all openly staring at each move I made, still not saying a word or showing any expression on their blank, wide-eyed faces.

At Grange I was feeling tired. I woke a man on a doorstep and asked him if there was somewhere I could camp for the night.

He drowsily told me that a farmhouse a few miles further on had a spare bed for travellers. Driving on I soon found the two-storeyed farmhouse and went in. The farmer—his upper lip twice the height of his lower—immediately flung open the door and said: 'Sure, and would you be coming inside.' I told him I would, if I was asked, and soon was shown a very clean and tidy but rough room. There was a second room lined with tin. This was a sort of washroom but there was neither water nor tub to be seen. They had never used it, but if I wanted to clean up I could drag in a tin dish and a bucket of water from the creek, to pour over myself as I sat in the dish. I explained I wasn't all that dirty having had a bath in Lancaster.

TEA was the most jolly event. It consisted of heaps of eggs, meat and damper, while the farmer, his wife, daughter and a housemaid gathered around examining me closely, and asking questions dating back roughly to the day I was born. They asked me how I liked Ireland and I told them I really hoped to come back. I was fascinated by the many long-eared dogs pulling carts along the road. The family went quiet when I commented on this. One hurried off to round up all the other farmer families within range to invite them over to meet *The Australian native.* The kitchen was crowded in no time. The usual drawings followed, using sheets of wrapping paper. After explaining that our natives couldn't read or write, I told them that anyone who needed to pass through the aboriginal reserves in Central Australia was required to obtain a permit. One lady asked, with a serious look on her face, 'And would ye now be tellin' us how the natives knew whether you had permits or not?' I was allowed to go to bed about midnight as they pointed out that I must be feeling a bit tired. Next morning, after a huge farm breakfast I asked what I owed, thinking of the $15 I'd spent on a night's accommodation in the States. The bill was 15/- and try as I did to give them more, they went in search of the exact change. The housemaid thought it was Christmas when I gave her a few shillings, and even that took a lot of persuasion. Just before I was about to get into the car amid the whole family who came out to see me off, the farmer secretly drew me aside and whispered with a twinkle in his eye, 'About those long-eared dogs, we really call them donkeys.'

As I drew near to Ballyshannon I saw a haystack travelling slowly along the road in front of me. There were no number plates or trafficators on it, just a bare haystack. It wasn't often I passed a haystack on the road and hoped it wouldn't turn right as I overtook it. I noticed a tiny donkey pulling a trolley so loaded with hay stooks that they dropped out onto the road. They completely obscured the little old farmer sitting on the trolley asleep against the stack behind him. It was certainly a peaceful change from Broadway.

Just before Londonderry, I picked up a farmer walking along dressed in a suit. I asked him where he was off to. He told me he was going to Derry and I asked him why. It was to the ceremony of the year to which everyone goes. I happened to be driving in to Derry on the day of the year it was being held!

The streets were empty. I drove down the main street and parked the car in the shade of some trees near a creek. By the time I walked back the streets were crammed with people. The arrival of the groups playing bagpipes parted the crowds, and their yelling increased to be heard over the pipes. It was bedlam and I was curious to know what it was all about. One screeching Irish girl paused for breath, so I asked her. She replied in a hysterical scream: 'We were liberated!'

Thinking they must have had some luck the night before, I asked her just when it was they were freed? She charged off into the yelling mob shrieking over her shoulder that it was in 1690. Apparently King William had chased away *the enemy* surrounding the town. He had given the people something to eat, and thus they were liberated. Today they were just as happy as they must have been on that day in 1690.

I was due in Stranraer that night so I raced off to Belfast, handed the car in and caught the train to Larne. The owners drove me to the railway station with the same car with which I had just driven 800 miles around Ireland. After another smooth crossing back over the Irish Sea, I climbed into the waiting car which took me to the mess and my bed at West Freugh.

Chapter 10

I TOOK THE LOW ROAD

'Mug of cocoa...'

THE Vauxhall was still safe and sound in its hangar. After breakfast, I pointed the car in the direction of Ayr, along the coast road of Scotland, adjoining the Firth of Clyde. June and Ron in Massachusetts had given me the address of some relatives of theirs in Mauchline, near Ayr. They were thus doomed to a visit; they had already been warned in writing. The Scottish accent was getting stronger with each mile I travelled north, and was rather fascinating to listen to. A padre from Woomera had been sending Christmas cards to a family living on a flourishing tomato farm for many years. He had written to them again, warning I might be calling in. They were the Aitkens of Lanark, on the way to Edinburgh, where I was due to see Sir John Evetts' son at the Redford Barracks.

The glass-houses full of tomato plants were heated by air piped from a huge brick furnace. He showed me over the whole farm. It was all he could do to persuade me to go out again into the freezing night air. Eventually we managed to reach the warm farmhouse for tea. There were visitors staying that evening and Mr Aitken was most upset that he did not have a bed for me, but after hearing of my bush life in Australia he conceded that I would survive. He nevertheless drove with me to make sure I found a bed at a friend's boarding house a few miles along the Edinburgh road.

Except for Belfast with its one-way traffic, Edinburgh seemed to me the next most complicated city which I had driven through. I was constantly being blocked off by police or No Entry signs, but somehow I managed to drive into Queens Street next to a paddock of the same name, in the shadow of Edinburgh Castle. This was built, of course, to ward off *the enemy*. Still having no fixed place of abode, I decided it was too late to ring Redford Barracks and went in search of a place to camp. One large two-storey farmhouse, a few miles out—with a prominent sign advertising bed and porridge—turned me away because I was on my own. It was difficult to wash only half a double bed sheet. I had heard about these Scots, but thinking it over, the other half of the sheet would still have been clean. It would have been a waste of soap to wash it.

This happened several times, as I drove in ever increasing circles around the town until I happened on a place six miles out, called Cramond Brig. It was on the road towards the bridge over the Firth of Forth. It had been hours since I had started this search. If this failed I would have to camp in the car, I concluded, as I beat on the heavy door. When it opened I shook hands with one of the jolliest men I had ever met, who called 'Och noo, coom on in mon to the wee fire we've got going.' I mentioned I was looking for somewhere to camp for the night and he assured me he would find me a room, even if it meant he and his wife sleeping in their coal cellar to leave their bed vacant. The little gathering of Scots around the fire welcomed me and the usual discourse on Australia began immediately. The jolly owner told me I'd be wanting something to eat so I sat alone in the dining room while a feast fit for Bonny Prince Charlie was brought in. My car had to be stored out of the night air, he insisted, so he moved several items in a barn under the hotel to make space for it. Later, I enquired why he called his place the Cramond Brig Hotel. He pointed to a stone bridge over a watercourse explaining that was a *brig,* and Cramond was nearby. The room he allotted me contained not one, but two huge double beds. I was soon asleep in one of them; he didn't mind the waste in cleaning both halves of the sheet.

In the morning, he brought me a mug of cocoa in bed. Going down into the breakfast room I accidentally discovered how to win friends. The girl cleaning the table smiled and another lady came in with a tray of porridge. She informed me the girl was her daughter, Ester. I replied that I thought they were sisters, upon which she said I would be welcome there anytime. Edinburgh Castle was the first establishment to examine, so I climbed up to the stone buildings, after extricating the car from the barn. It was uncanny the way all those rocks balanced on the hill. *The enemy* would have had quite a job getting near the castle walls. The view over the cannon in the battlements took in the whole of Edinburgh and the Firth of Forth. Once outside again and back at Queens Park at the base of the hill, I ran into more bagpipes than I had seen in my life, all playing at once. I had always been very keen on them, even before I had made a bag out of kangaroo skin in the bush. I wandered about through the pipers, each of a different clan, rehearsing for the Edinburgh Festival in just over a week's time. In each group an old piper would creep around the circle with his eyes closed listening to each player. When he detected one to be out of tune—if that's what they call it—he would touch him gently on the shoulder. That player knew his drones would be checked later.

Another Scottish friend at Woomera had made me promise to call in to see Tom and Dixie Steele the moment I got to Edinburgh. I phoned them from the box in Queens Park. They had also been expecting me and told me to come straight over. They gave me directions from Queens Park even though I had not mentioned where I was calling from. After replacing the receiver, I decided they might have known by the sound of the bagpipes surrounding the call box. Sure enough, the newspaper story from Adelaide was there on the table, having been sent by their Woomera relation. After tea, followed by a conducted tour of the town, I returned to the 'sisters' at Cramond Brig to stay once more.

Being near to the Forth Bridge, which I had seen in picture books since I had started school, I drove out to see it closely for the first time. I was surprised to see it was built only for trains. Trying to manoeuvre the car into a position for a photo, I became hopelessly bogged. I needed all my skills gained in Australia to get moving again.

Holyroodhouse was the next call in Edinburgh I had been strongly advised to make. I found that Mary Queen of Scots had slept on a bed made out of solid concrete covered by a thin sheet. Admittedly, it was built in the 16th century, before inner-spring mattresses had been invented, but even straw would have been an improvement on the concrete. Two little girls named Maureen and Mary had drawn my attention to it, as one of them had rapped it with her knuckles, which she almost broke. She lifted the sheet and told her friend it seemed a 'bit hard.' It was at that stage I saw the rock slab. The attendant had chastised them bitterly for daring to touch the historic four-poster, so they appealed to me for protection. Maureen and Mary stayed with me for the duration of the inspection and offered to show me every place of interest nearby. They had lived in Edinburgh for all of their nine years. We went to a craggy hill known as King Arthur's Seat. After the concrete bed, I gathered the royalty of early Scotland didn't worry much about their personal comfort. The time came for my two little friends to be driven to their home, after which I phoned Colonel Evetts at the Redford Barracks.

He told me to lose no time in visiting the Barracks and that all his officers were there in the mess to greet me. I changed my belt for a prismatic compass case strap I carried for such special occasions. I transferred the knife and watch pouches to it

Redford Barracks is the home of the Royal Scots Fusiliers, but during the time of my visit they were undergoing an amalgamation with another group. Everyone was pleased as fury with the operation. I learned that a *Fusil* is a light musket which works rather like a capgun and fusiliers were the ones who carried them about. Although fusils have gone somewhat out of date, the name still remains.

The guard had been instructed to let me through. Soon after I pulled up outside the grey headquarters building. Colonel Evetts came out and ushered me through the cold stone arches and up to the officers' lounge room.

A group of about eight officers rose stiffly and I was introduced to them in turn, starting with Lieutenant Ramrod. They were forced to rise stiffly as they were all wearing long skin-tight tartan trousers with swords hanging from polished belts. Coloured rope looped over their shoulders to hang in tassels like shaving brushes, over rows of clanking medals. Toothbrush moustaches completed the scene, as did the addition of the occasional monocle. The swords made the hunting knife on my compass case belt seem very small indeed.

I discovered the trousers they wore are known as 'trews' which compel the wearer to move as if each of his legs were inside lengths of six-inch bore casing. The lounge floor was covered by thick carpet into which sank deep leather chairs. The place had an atmosphere of discipline, tradition and ceremony. I decided that either the atmosphere or I had to be adjusted if I were to get anywhere, so I greeted Lieutenant Ramrod as I would an Australian. The frosty, barely perceptible inclination of his head was the only acknowledgment I received, as he stood rigidly to attention, being the youngest officer present. Even so, his sword trailed on the ground. Captain Cutlass bowed slightly from where his bore casing left off. His medals tinkled back into place when he straightened up. In Major Monocle I saw a possible ally. He seemed much jollier and replied to anything I said with a 'by gad!' His eyebrows raised, releasing his eyeglass to dangle on the end of a length of black string. It just missed being broken on the handle of his sword each time, and I idly wondered why he didn't wear it in the other eye. I had never seen one of these before, except in pictures. I thought they would be handy to keep cinders out of one eye at least, while travelling on Queensland trains.

After the introductions, ending with Lieutenant Colonel Iceberg, I began to wonder what they thought I looked like in my desert boots. I had a feeling that perhaps *I* might be the one who was different. By the way they looked at me I gathered mine was like no other uniform *they* had ever seen.

I began answering questions about Australia, relating stories about Colonel Evetts' father—the General—in the deserts around Woomera, and how he had survived the wilds out there. They were all still standing and I was looking more frequently towards the leather chairs. I stepped up to Captain Cutlass to examine his sword handle. I noted how well they made things in 1066. At last a discreet titter rippled through the officers and I soon found them to be a 'Jolly decent bunch of chaps,' to quote Major Monocle. All except Lieutenant Ramrod—who was a junior officer—and must have felt he should not relax too much in the presence of the Colonel. I decided to try to cheer him up, as even Lieutenant Colonel Iceberg had thawed. I directed my answers mainly towards him, standing in his gleaming hob-nailed boots, impeccable right up to his silky smooth white face. I was sure he'd be O.K. if I could only break up that geometrical expression.

Just after I had suggested we all sit down the Colonel asked if someone would press the button for the orderly. In a microsecond a Corporal materialised, to stand like a statue holding a large silver tray. Being the guest, I was asked first what I'd have to drink. I turned to the Corporal and told him I'd like a mug of cocoa. A deathly silence followed, broken finally by the Major's exclamation of 'By gad!' He let his monocle fall out of his eye and it became tangled in the coloured rope. The Corporal's control was remarkable, but victory was gained as I noticed Lieutenant Ramrod's geometrical lips curl into a smile. After that, the rest was easy and everyone asked for cocoa, which was not the done thing in this place.

Soon we were all sitting around with our cocoa, and I continued with yarns about the bush. I'm sure this had never happened before in Redford Barracks. Everyone who visits the Barracks is required to inspect the silverware. It is all kept on shelves in darkened cellars and is in the form of cups, trays and vases. They are wonderfully carved and engraved and are part of the tradition of the place. It is added to from time to time and has been with them for donkeys years. My time had apparently come; the orderly had collected the cocoa mugs and Colonel Evetts led the way through the hushed passages to the silver room. Each piece of silver was reverently handed to me while its history was explained fully. I thought it would be as much as my life was worth to have dropped a piece. Halfway through the ritual Major Monocle drew me aside and whispered: 'I say, awfully sorry to do this to you, old chap, but I really can't do a thing about it.' He was, just as I thought, an ally, but at the same time I really was interested. One large hand-hammered silver bucket would have been just the thing for collecting rainwater for car batteries.

I mentioned that I had an arrangement to visit the theodolite factory in York the following day. They all discussed the best ways I could get there, a hundred miles away. The result was that I left my car at the Barracks, where one of the staff cars would be available to drive me to the railway station and collect me on my return, proving what a really decent bunch they were.

After a wonderful dinner in the mess, followed by more hot cocoa and tales from the mulga woods, I returned to Cramond Brig to sleep, where the jolly old Scot at the hotel was expecting me. He sounded like Harry Lauder the way he laughed and slapped his knee when I told him about my day, and I thought I should take pity on him—after he choked on a breath when I told him about the cocoa.

THE next day I hurried to Redford Barracks, wondering what reception the next visitor from Australia might expect, and left the car at the Colonel's 'Alma House.' A staff car appeared immediately and the young driver leaped out and opened the door for me, clicking the steel heels of his glittering hob-nailed boots. On the way to the station I discovered he only knew the one word 'Sir' and was as rigid as ever, despite all my efforts to brighten him

up in so short a time. He drew up at the railway station and again
opened the door for me. He was really quite a nice sort of boy,
and I thanked him and told him how good he had been. I walked
over to buy a ticket to York with his one solitary word still ringing
in my ears.

I was surprised to see the Sydney Harbour Bridge over a creek
as we steamed through Newcastle. Eventually I boarded a bus to
take me to the hotel which had been booked for me by the Cooke,
Troughton & Simms instrument people. I asked the conductress
to let me know when we arrived at the *Hind Quarter of Beef Hotel*.
She looked blank, as if she had not heard of it, although she told
me she had lived in York all her life. I found the letter from the
company in my survey bag, and the reason for her blank
expression became immediately apparent. It was the *Shoulder of
Mutton Hotel,* and soon after I was installed in my room. I soon left
for a hike into York for a look around.

I edged myself into one street by standing sideways. It was the
narrowest street I had ever seen. The shops had balconies which
allowed people upstairs to hand things easily across the road. In
one place I found I could walk with my shoulders cleaning the
windows on both sides at the same time. At the end of the street I
saw that it was called, appropriately, *The Shambles*.

Back at the *Shoulder of Mutton* for tea, I discovered letters
waiting for me from Jimmy Stewart and Qantas concerning my
return trip to Australia. The letters had been re-directed to the
hotel by my friends in Edinburgh as they knew this to be the date
of my arranged inspection of the factory. I had always known how
thoroughly reliable the British were with their great emphasis on
detail.

After tea a man introduced himself as Brian Payne, the optical
manager of the instrument factory. He invited me to his place for
coffee. His son, David, was the most interested boy I'd met,
asking questions about Australia, at machine-gun rate, and at
eleven years of age his queries were surprisingly intelligent. The
evening was, therefore, taken up with sketching for him. A year
later I was to receive a sixteen-page account from David about a
holiday trip he had taken. It was set out in such detail he even

described such things as how he opened the car door and on which side he sat.

Finally, David fell asleep. I told Brian that he had helped make the theodolite I had used in the desert for many years. It had been one of the items which I'd relied on for my survival.

He drove me back to the hotel, advising me he would be there early in the morning to take me on a conducted tour of the old established firm of the Cooke, Troughton & Simms. I had used instruments which had been made by them a hundred years before.

Soon after breakfast Brian had me in his car driving to the works which I had been so keen on seeing since I was David's age. From the casting of the instruments in the foundry, I was conducted through each stage to the finished product. I walked through the circle-dividing equipment, the spirit level grinding machines, lathes turning precision axes and optical sections for the telescopes. I knew I would have been the envy of many surveyors in Australia for this opportunity. I was allowed to photograph any section I wanted, and the resulting slides were shown to many interested groups later in Australia. One particular slide was always greatly appreciated. I wondered what was so exceptional about it, as it only showed a machine for optically lining-up prisms. I asked one group what they particularly liked about the picture and was immediately asked if I was kidding. Someone then pointed out the calendar on a wall in the background. It showed a picture of a well-proportioned girl ready for a swim, a feature I hadn't noticed at the time.

I went to one lady assembling the parts of a tripod, and thanked her for helping to save my life. She looked up and stifled a yawn as she replied 'That's all right, luv.' One man had been at the same bench for 45 years, making the leather cases and carrying straps for the instrument boxes. I'm sure a leather worker could not be found anywhere to equal this old craftsman. I had carried many of the products of his work up mountains while surveying.

The carpenters making the dovetailed boxes for the instruments would have been most upset if they had seen my own woodwork on tucker boxes in the bush. I didn't dare tell them what had happened to one of their beautifully-made theodolite boxes on one project. A surveyor had moved his instrument and tripod from where he had left the box among the saltbush and a Caterpillar D8 bulldozer had backed slowly over it, converting it to matchsticks in seconds.

After lunch in the official dining room and upon completion of the tour, Brian drove me to his home for tea. We had a slide show of my aboriginal friends from Australia. The slides were again so welcome that I was glad I had brought them along.

One more night at the *Shoulder of Mutton* and I was back on the train to Edinburgh. I rang Redford Barracks for the promised staff car, so that I could collect the Vauxhall. It had been a truly worthwhile visit. After a cheerful farewell from Lieutenant Ramrod, Captain Cutlass, Major Monocle and Colonel Iceberg—with thanks to Colonel Evetts for his wonderful help—I stopped in Princes Street just long enough to send two tartan rugs home to Australia.

It was time to be carrying on with the main attack into Scotland. This had to begin with the old barge called *Queens Ferry* to transport the car over the Firth of Forth. As I drove past Cramond Brig I was very tempted to call in, but knowing that would mean staying the night, I reluctantly decided against it.

I was to regret this decision later in the evening when I found there was nowhere in Perth to camp. I thought a lot about Cramond Brig, as I lay doubled up on a lounge chair in a hotel lobby a little before midnight at Blairgowrie.

Chapter 11

HEATHER, PEAT AND HONEY

U PON studying a map of Scotland I decided on a counter-clockwise direction of attack from Edinburgh, because I was wondering how I could cross all the creeks on the western side. One big creek threatened to cut Scotland in half, from Fort William to Inverness, and went under the names of Loch Linnhe, Loch Lochy and Loch Ness. The stories I had heard of this last one were rather like tales of the bunyip.

It was not until I drew near Balmoral Castle that the effects on my back of the lounge chair at Blairgowrie began to ease. A flag flying from a pole on the battlements of the castle indicated the Queen was in residence awaiting a royal birth.

Two German girl hitchhikers stopped me at Balmoral for a lift to Aberdeen. As they only spoke the language of their fatherland, I could have been on my own for all that was said between us.

Judging by the signs they made, I gathered they were grateful when we drove into Aberdeen. They unloaded their mansize packs, shouldered them as if they were full of feathers, and hiked off. I climbed back into the car still panting from the effort of lifting them out of the trunk, and drove via Nairn to Inverness. On the way two army recruits on an exercise begged for a ride to rest their soft feet from their shining hob-nailed military boots. No sooner had they 'de-bussed', a boy of twelve—as round as he was high—clambered into their place for a lift into town. He obviously had not done enough hiking as he could barely fit through the door. As he spread out covering the place occupied by the two recruits, I was pushed tightly against the opposite side able only to breathe out. We stopped near another pair of girls hitchhiking. As he oozed out onto the road I found I was able to breathe in for a change. One of the girls, sitting on a pack, saw the scene and came over to ask if they could have a help along with their tour.

I felt as if I was driving a bus, but being only too pleased to meet all these people, I replied in my best Australian accent 'Right-o, glad to, hop in.' Without another word they looked at each other and began laughing. I wondered what the joke was, and when they finally stopped laughing, they informed me they too were from Australia and hadn't heard an Aussie accent for months. When I told them I was off to John O'Groats, Ullapool and back to Inverness where we were at present, they leaped into the car and stayed there for the next three days. The best they had hoped for was a few hours ride.

It took only five minutes to discover that they were Pat and Pam and that one of them lived in New South Wales, quite near to my sister. As we drove on, to my surprise, the other girl began to cry bitterly. Her friend explained that this happened every time she remembered she had broken her camera not long before, and was thus unable to take home pictures of her trip. I could well understand her plight, so resigned myself to a moist trip through Scotland, depending on how often she thought about the camera.

They told me they had been wanting to camp in a castle at least once. One they had in mind was Carbisdale Castle; it contained a youth hostel and was more or less on our way. Being only too pleased to help, I readily offered to include this on our trip. We discovered it had been built to keep out *the enemy* with wall-slots, drawbridge and all, commanding an overall view of the valley below. A mountain fog was rolling in, hiding a creek from view. I found I could stay there too. To avoid a second night of coiling up to sleep—with thoughts of knights in shining armour, desert boots and hunting knives on their belts—I charged in over the drawbridge with the girls. The castle was full of holiday hitchhikers all talking at once, and I thought of how peaceful it had been on the Nullarbor Plain back in Australia. Pam forgot all about the camera for a while and raced about the battlements as though she'd lived there all her life. As a tireless organiser, she proved to have no equal in the group. She catapulted into rooms at odd times to collect everyone to share in her latest discoveries in the dungeons. Even here a man's home could not be really called his castle.

The drawbridge was still down over the moat the next morning: an indication that we hadn't been attacked during the night by *the enemy*. This saved a swim back to the Vauxhall, in which we were soon heading via Wick to John O'Groats. The castle was soon lost to us in the swirling mist. It occurred to me just how brisk it must have been living there, centuries before, in the dank, rock-lined rooms, getting up at all hours to fire arrows through the slots at the tin-clad visitors. A dreadful ear-shattering noise told us we were at the most north-easterly corner of Scotland. On investigation I found several compressed-air tanks, each the size of a boiler on a locomotive, coupled to funnel-shaped foghorns. This gave out the melody advising ships to not become impaled on pointed rocks jutting out of the sea—if they could possibly avoid it. How the keeper stood this monotonous row, night and day, was hard to imagine. It all sounded like a mob of bull camels roaring into microphones.

There was a cliff, famous for being the most northern part of the mainland, known as Dunnett Head. This was the most northerly spot visited on my trip around the world. To soothe the sobbing Pam, who'd remembered her camera, we made the trek to it. Later we drove off between prairies of dry peat cut into slabs.

It was lifted out of trenches to dry, in paddocks of heather. Peat and Heather seemed to get along very well together.

We saw the great white sphere of the atomic establishment of Doonreay. Although I would have known some people there, I was not able to call in.

A little building at Reay had a sign: *meals*. The jolly Scotswoman who ran the place had a bright twinkle in her eye, and gave me rather a shock when we went in for tea. On learning of the hitchhikers and myself being quite separate parties, she pointed out to me emphatically as she went into the kitchen, that I 'would be marrying one of them.' I immediately thought about the ultimatum I was issued with at the Blarney Stone and how all these people seemed to dislike seeing me so happy. Nevertheless, it made me feel quite uneasy, especially when another woman appeared from the kitchen and agreed with her sister.

That night I left my passengers at the Youth Hostel, shown on their list to be near a village named Tongue. Promising to call for them in the morning, I drove off to a farm I had noticed with a *bed and breakfast* sign outside the cow yard. The lady showed me the room set aside for anyone who had read the sign, explaining that her husband was at present working on the Isle of Skye. Her kiddies—or *bairns*—helped her with the chores. Everything was spotlessly clean and the farm supper she served was perfect. I told them about Australia and the waterless deserts, aborigines and kangaroos. Soon I had a pencil and pad upon which I drew pictures about my home country until midnight. I drew bony dingoes, 'roos, piccaninnies, aborigines' camps and even the Sydney Harbour Bridge. The children were sitting on my knees, lap and shoulder, while their mother preserved each sketch carefully. The family had never been anywhere but Tongue. When the chance came, I mentioned that the bairns could do with a survey trim, to which they all agreed. We had a spell from the Art Department, and I cut their hair with my clippers from the 'Igh' 'Ob'n bag by the warmth of the kitchen fire.

It was one of the most pleasant nights I had spent anywhere, listening to Alistair's excited Scottish accent, as he talked about the pictures. Months after I had returned to Australia, I received a letter postmarked 'Tongue,' containing a greeting card wee Alistair had drawn especially for me. Needless to say, a return letter was on its way within the day.

After porridge and farm eggs I was ordered to collect the girls from the hostel and return to the farm immediately for a 'wee cup of tea.' It was then onwards to Durness, over moors close to the north-western corner of Scotland. We then turned south to Ullapool. There was fresh water everywhere, trickling about the mountains. Peat was still in the paddocks—with heather—in some of the most wonderful country in Scotland. The sheep looked more like mobile mops, with their wool dragging along the ground like a council road sweeping machine, but at least they seemed quite warm.

ULLAPOOL, on the banks of Loch Broom, was the scene of much fishing from the jetty. After leaving the girls at the youth hostel, I met a keen Scottish angler, aged eight. He insisted I come with him for a lesson, after I mentioned I had caught one fish in my life in Massachusetts. That was all right until next morning—when his day started—at 4.30 a.m.

I was still half asleep when I collected Pat and Pam to carry on to Inverness. On the way they forced me to help in cornering a 'council street sweeper' sheep for a photograph. They had no success: it took on the agility of a mountain goat making for the highlands. Delivering them to friends back in Inverness at last, I was thanked and told we might meet again in Australia. Feeling a little scared, I hurried off south-westerly towards Loch Ness to take my chances with the monster. It had been a drier trip than I'd thought: Pam hadn't brought her lost camera to mind as often as I had feared.

Barely half an hour had elapsed before I saw on the road in front three enormous packs weaving along. I slowed down to see what was making them move, and three girls turned around and waved. Stopping my passenger bus once more, I began to ask if I could help at all. Before I had finished they were already unlooping the straps from their shoulders. I jumped out, trying to appear casual. They asked then if I was going to Fort William and if so, could I give them and their wee packs a lift. I told them I'd be honoured to, as I opened up the trunk in which I installed their loads, an operation which all but upended the car. As we drove, once again all our histories were re-told. I discovered they lived in Glasgow and were on their way home after their hitchhiking holiday. I learned that the blonde one was Sheila, the raven-haired one was Moira and the one in between was Patricia. Their ages averaged twenty and their accent was a real pleasure to listen to. They in turn were intrigued at the bush yarns I was able to tell, because one asked 'Och, and tell us about the wee kangaroos.'

In no time we were driving along the banks of Loch Ness where in return I pleaded 'Och, and tell me about the wee monster.' I couldn't really see how you could have a 'wee monster' as the two words had opposite meanings but they laughed at my attempt to speak like them. We stopped for a photograph of the Loch, of course, throwing a stone in first to cause ripples as 'the thing' submerged. It was good for a story back home, anyway, and the girls helped with the joke by each throwing a stone in at the same time, to show where the coils went under as well.

The castle on the banks of the loch was at least built to keep off a real enemy. It was named Urquhart Castle. I thought it was a good job that it wasn't snowing on any inhabitants, as it had no roof.

Past Fort William we crossed another loch by ferry. This was near Glencoe, where—on paying the operator five shillings and sixpence—we were told the famous Battle of Glencoe had occurred. As the area consisted mostly of water, I thought that by the time it was over the armour must have been quite rusty.

A bridge over a loch near Oban cost another five shillings to cross. Soon the girls were installed in their youth hostel. Plans for a lift to Fort William had long since vanished, when I said I would be going through Glasgow. They were filled with glee to have the chance of a ride right home. I was equally as pleased to have the company of the jolliest of lassies. As it turned out I was sorry I hadn't stayed at their youth hostel. I might have been stretching the 'youth' a bit, but they did admit other old folk.

That night was one of the few times it rained since I had left the Nullarbor Plains. I sloshed about Oban trying to find a place to camp. I must have driven twenty miles around the outskirts, and was resigned to sleeping on the front seat of the car, when I discovered a bed and breakfast establishment. A woman of ninety came to the door—which creaked like the Glencoe armour—and showed me to a room. Lumps of plaster kept falling off the walls, held back from hitting the bed by dirty torn wallpaper. The bed sank in the middle, bending the occupant into the shape of a boomerang.

There was no bathroom, except a cracked jug in a broken basin on a marble slab, which I thought I could sleep on if the bed proved impossible. Asking for a towel or rag to dry my face after a shave, she looked at me as if I were eccentric. She grudgingly gave me a torn towel, mumbling at the same time that it would be sixpence extra on my bill. I wished I had been back at the hostel. I was sure I would not be able to eat her breakfast in the morning. Outside, I saw volumes of water surging up out of the road, indicating a burst main. I was glad to have something to do, so I hiked to the council building and advised them about it. Before long trucks and men were gouging into the bubbling water to make the repairs. It seemed to be in keeping with my bedroom.

Next morning could not come quickly enough. I had only straightened out a little by the time I got to the hostel to collect the girls. The marble slab had proved too short.

Struggling into the pouring rain with their packs, I placed them into the trunk before going in once again to ask if the girls were ready. They had been overjoyed to see me, thinking perhaps that I might not have returned. Soon we were all driving away from that otherwise wonderful little settlement by the Firth of Lorne. They were all very angry about the old woman's treatment of me, imploring me not to take her as an example of Scottish hospitality, which, of course, I didn't anyway.

We drove easterly now. I was quite determined to drive along the bonny banks of Loch Lomond.

I asked the girls which was the high road and which was the low road. I deduced the low one would have put us closer to the water level, which was where I wanted to be. They laughed at my eagerness, as they had lived all their lives near this famous loch. On the way, Moira—who had taken Sheila's place in the front seat—turned around and asked 'Patricia, and did ye get the wee jar of honey?' To which she received an affirmative reply. Then in the most musical and most pleasant accent, which I've often since tried to emulate without any success, she continued 'and was it heather honey?' She then went on to say 'Och! and could I have a wee look at the wee map?' I finally asked why it was they always started off each sentence by sounding as if somebody had jabbed a needle into them? The tears were running down their faces by the time they had stopped laughing, explaining the expression was the same as I often said 'Oh!'

It was still raining heavily as we stopped on the bank opposite Ben Lomond, a 3,000-foot high mountain. We could just see its foothills through the mist. We had some dinner in the car. The wind rocked the car on its springs, but at least we were dry. After lunch, the girls asked for some sketches of Australia. Pencil and paper were produced, and I drew up the things I thought they, as school teachers, might find of interest to show their pupils. Upon handing over the last sketch of them trudging along the road with their packs at Loch Ness, they informed me that they now had a present for me in return. Upon opening the box I found a polished wooden shield with a metal coat of arms with the words 'Gang Warily' cast in relief. It had a tartan square of the Drummond clan to remember them by. I was then told the meaning of the words which meant 'Go warily.' They had bought the present for me in Oban. I was instructed to carry it with me in my Land Rover on the lone expeditions I did in the Australian deserts. I have it still, as a treasured possession on my wall, with my memories of Loch Lomond as vivid and pleasant as ever.

During this stop the rain eased, so we climbed out to see some fast-flowing rapids, which spilled into the loch. After a photograph of the scene with my three passengers sitting on a rock, we moved on. At last I plucked up the courage to ask them to sing the song for me in this appropriate setting. I realised how close to the present situation the words were. That was when they

got to the lines about parting and I again became a little uneasy when they all looked at me as they sang the verse:
For me and my true love will never meet again ...
They seemed to enjoy seeing me squirm, knowing my lonely bush background.

After another photo at Luss, with Loch Lomond in the background, and an inspection of a little old church, we all found ourselves on the outskirts of Glasgow. As things familiar to them came into view, each in turn would gesticulate excitedly.

We drove through the glistening wet streets of Glasgow to Sheila's house, where I unloaded her pack and took it in. We all stayed for an early evening meal, thanks to Sheila's mother. After that, we carried on again to Jordan Hill Drive to take Moira home. I met her father, who was a ship's pilot on the Clyde. I discovered that the girls were going to the Edinburgh Festival, having arrived home in time. I had unfortunately indicated I'd be heading south through the Lake District. Although I could have headed south after seeing the Festival, and given my friends a lift there too, I had to admit to myself I was too shy to change my plans.

Patricia was the last to return home. After finding a room in a hotel for myself I drove her for miles through the wet slippery streets to her house. I returned to the hotel quickly, before I forgot the way. I was feeling suddenly quite lonely as I sat in my room: much more so than in Central Australia. So I wrote some letters home and climbed up to my bed, which was at least four feet from the floor. I wondered how anyone who hadn't recently been climbing about the highlands after sheep, ever made it to the bed.

After falling asleep I dreamed of monsters and wee jars of heather honey, the latter with *Moira* on them. I almost changed my mind the next day. The rain had gone and it was bright and sunny once more, but I just couldn't remember where Jordan Hill was.

Chapter 12

GOODBYE PICCADILLY

THE road through the Lake District, passing through the most perfect country, compensated for not seeing the Edinburgh Festival. The day had gone all too quickly when I drove into a Yorkshire village called Masham. It was close to what looked on the map to be the middle of England. It consisted of a village square surrounded by old limestone buildings. The first boarding establishment was full so the landlady directed me to another across the square. I knocked on the stout oak door, nearly breaking my knuckles in the process. A happy lady came out and ushered me up to the room. She ordered me not to rise in the morning until she had brought my breakfast to me in bed. I told her I never had been used to eating while still in my swag roll, so I'd really rather get up if allowed. She didn't know what a swag was, but reluctantly consented, after which I accompanied her downstairs where a television set was operating.

Ordering me to sit down and watch, she walked back to the door, did an about turn and charged back into the room. She landed on the sofa in a flying leap, during which she twisted in mid-air. She ended up the right way for viewing the picture. She was at least 55 years of age and I idly wondered if I could do the same thing if I tried. This performance was repeated every time she got up to see to her stove, giving me an indication of just how strong the sofa must have been.

Passing through Leeds and Sheffield at noon on the following day, I found I could barely plough through the surging mass of people with the Vauxhall, as they poured out of the factories for dinner.

The next goal was Solihull, which was the town I was personally indebted to for making the Landrover. I had been using one of these vehicles only a few months before in Central Australia. It had brought me out of the desert safely, to embark on this trip. Once at Solihull I found myself a private hotel. Although it was very busy, the owners kindly arranged with a family from the town to look after me; they had made similar arrangements in the past. I had to pass the Rover factory on the way. I found the people at the hotel were really wonderful. I begged them to forgo their television programmes in order to see my slides of Australia. I was fast becoming tired of these slides, but realised they were new to each audience. Early next day saw me in Colonel Pogmore's office, the chief engineer at the plant, who was expecting me as a result of the telephone calls made from Aldermaston. He started by sending me in the company of a mechanical engineer to view their proving ground some miles away. We couldn't find a Rover car in the whole factory to drive in, so went in a Morris instead. As we drove, I wondered what the testing site would be like in comparison to where I took their vehicles in the bush. After driving around the course myself in a test vehicle, I was more than satisfied by the rigours of the tests. A complete guided tour of the works and engine factory reassured me that I was safe in relying, as I did, on these vehicles for my life.

Optical section – with bather in background – Cooke, Troughton & Simms, York.

Sheila, Pat and Moira with the trusty Vauxhall, north Scotland.

Sheila, Pat and Moira at falls near Loch Lomond.

The hitchhikers and a Scottish village scene.

Urquhart Castle and Loch Ness.

*Northern-most coast, Dunnet Head,
Scotland.*

The bubble car and TV repair van, Stratford-upon-Avon.

Harrison's chronometer,
(H-1, completed 1737) National
Maritime Museum, Greenwich.

It's a long way down...Eiffel Tower, Paris.

Statue of Joan of Arc, Paris.

Austrian village church.

Matterhorn.

Taxi and bus on Grand Canal, Venice.

End of the day, Sounion, Greece.

Artificial moon and Treetops, Kenya.

Baboon contemplating the author, Kenya.

It seemed impossible to be so close to Stratford-upon-Avon and not visit the house where Shakespeare wrote all the things which had plagued me throughout my school life. After leaving Solihull, I soon found myself outside Shakespeare's mother's house. Her 'carriage port' had quite a lean on it I noticed, before I crossed over a creek named the Avon, to stand outside William's house. A television repair van was parked outside, next to a bubble car. I thought of how much school work I would have been saved had they been there during his time. Anne Hathaway's house looked very like a large haystack with its heavily thatched roof.

Driving through Banbury once again, I looked up a friend, whose address I had been given while in Dover. He lived at Bletchley. I drove into the gravel track to stop outside a mansion. Helen and Bill Makinson came out and, as I'd been expected, no introductions were necessary. Bill was the manager of the Link Trainer Plant where mock-ups of cockpits were made for every type of aircraft. You could start the engines, take off, bank and land without leaving the stand upon which the trainer was bolted. I camped with them, after Bill had shown me the plant. A crowd of his friends arrived that night, once again to see the well-worn slides of Australia's outback. He was probably as tired of the factory as I was of the slides, but we both enjoyed what the other had to show.

A phone call to Cambridge failed to locate our old Chief Superintendent for the rocket range project. He had served his term in Australia, including a few desert camps with me, and had returned to his home here. I was then away to Southend-on-Sea where some friends from the atomic bomb trials were also expecting me. Foulness was the next port of call, to see Ron and Joyce Johnston. I had used Ron's particular 'scientist's hair style' on a Christmas card I had drawn for the atomic project. I noticed he was still wearing it—with not one hair out of place. The bush slides became a little more worn during the stay with them, after which I headed off westerly again to London.

AUSTRALIA House had some mail waiting for me, which was very welcome. I phoned Jimmy and Kay Stewart from there. Meeting Jim at his office in London, I followed him and his car through countless traffic jams back to Northwood. By the time we arrived at his house, I had sufficiently recovered from the surprise I received at Australia House: one of my letters had a Glasgow postmark. It was from Moira, who was describing her visit to the Edinburgh Festival, and I thought Jordan Hill might not have been so difficult to find after all.

Kay welcomed us and the evening was spent relating events of my expedition. It concluded with Jimmy, trying in vain to teach me how to say 'Och! and is it heather honey?' An itinerary had been worked out by Jimmy for my return trip back to Australia. The following day had to be spent in London, being injected for cholera and yellow fever, organising a permit to go to Africa, and a visa for Ceylon. I was quite sure Columbus didn't have to go through all this before his trips.

I had been instructed to buy a suit in London by everyone at Woomera, as they had never seen me dressed in anything but shorts. A day later, I went to a place suggested by Jimmy to see what I could find. I didn't know what I was going to do with the suit, but it would make others happy. After leaving the Vauxhall at my old faithful car park at Bedford Square, I hiked down Kingsway to the Strand.

A large sign advised me that I was outside the *Savoy Tailors Guild*, so I trudged in, still wearing my desert boots and open-necked shirt, with sleeves rolled up. It was still very hot and humid in London. The rain at Loch Lomond was all I was to see for the rest of my trip. A small polite man came over to me and inquired if he could be of assistance. I asked if he happened to have a suit he could sell me. His rimless pince-nez glasses almost fell off as he controlled himself and asked me to follow him. My question seemed a little redundant I found, as we went down a flight of stairs to land in a sea of suits, hanging row upon row along every wall. I told him I had never bought a suit before. He asked me first what colour I preferred. He showed me through shelves of material and I selected one which reminded me of the blackened results of a bush fire. When he asked me what style I had in mind, I could only reply that one with a waistcoat would be handy, to save carrying my watch in a belt pouch. He glanced down at the hunting knife and big brass buckle on the belt, and hastened to ensure me he could supply the appropriate garment. With that, he took a coat at random to try it for size. When I put it on my arms protruded out of the sleeves ten inches at least, and the front would not meet. So he tried another. This one almost broke across the back as I leant forward, so another was tried. He beamed and told me it was perfect, but I pointed out that the arms were too narrow, making it impossible for me to be able to roll them up. The next one felt just right. It had a tag tied to the sleeve button and when I tried to read it, he made a grab for it. He tried to hide the label, but when I finally read it I noticed the word printed across it: *Portly*. In between my spasms of laughing, I told him I had never been called portly before, upon which he wrung his little white hands as he explained the sign didn't refer to the customer, but simply to the tailor's description of the cut. I told him not to worry as it was quite a good joke.

The waistcoat came to light next. After installing the watch from my belt pouch in the pocket, and hooking my thumbs in the armholes trying to look *portly* I saw him almost in tears. I quickly returned the watch to the belt and took it all off, saying it felt all right and I would take it. I asked him if he sold accessories for suits. He visibly brightened up, assuring me that they stocked everything so I asked him if I could have a pair of *bowyangs* to match. His face fell once more and he admitted he had to ask what they were. He had never heard of them in a lifetime of tailoring. I explained that they fitted below the knees and were bands to keep the bottoms of the trousers out of the mud while shovelling. He began whimpering in a funny way again, suggesting he must have had an unhappy life. I advised him that I could make a pair myself out of water-bag straps.

By now several other shop assistants had assembled and he began parcelling up the precious suit in tissue paper. I asked if I could have it sent. He replied that their service extended to anywhere in the world, and as an after-thought asked me the one question 'Australia?' I was amazed and asked how he knew I came from there. He looked at me intelligently and explained that he had just guessed it.

As I walked away along the Strand towards Trafalgar Square, I turned around to see a bunch of faces leaning out of the door of the unfortunate *Savoy Tailors Guild* staring after me. I wondered what the matter was: I had already paid for the suit. I collected the suit in Adelaide on my return and still have it—unworn—but for the fitting in the shop.

'...*seems a bit small.*'

THAT day was the one scheduled by a member of Parliament I had met near Bristol, for me to visit the Big Ben clock tower. I was there on time for the guide to take me up, after he had examined my card of introduction. We climbed up the 350 stairs to the works of the famous clock, where I have an idea I may have disappointed the guide. I said the assembly of gears looked like a boring plant back home. It was quite an experience, nevertheless, to see what motivated the clock known to everyone in the world. He showed me the back of one of the face pieces, after which we went up to the bell itself. *Big Ben* is the name given to the bell, and we were within a foot of the hammers when they rung out their familiar tune, after which they struck three o'clock. By the time it was all over I was thankful I wasn't there at 12. Taking out my watch I noted that we both had exactly the same time.

Two days later, I was due to meet George at the Farnborough Air show. He had arranged an official ticket for me. That night I received a phone call at Jimmy's from the nurse friend from Australia, inviting me back to Bristol for a farewell visit. She asked if she could make the trip from London with me in the car, which we arranged on the spot. The next night saw us both back at their place at Richmond Hill.

As good as it was to see them again, I once more had to leave in the foggy early hours of the morning in order to be in Farnborough in time for the show. Bristol to Farnborough wasn't far by Australian standards, but in the fog proved quite a journey. Near Aldershot I saw two men carrying a piano on straps looped around their shoulders. They were transporting it from a van into a house. I pulled up and enquired if I was anywhere near Farnborough. They explained at great length how to arrive at the first of the advisory signs, erected specially for the Air Show. They did this without putting down the piano. Soon I was making use of my official car sticker, within the boundaries of a parking area near the aerodrome.

Somehow I found George and we both went to view the aircraft on the tarmac. One jet plane sighted from behind looked like a large pair of binoculars. If walls had been erected around the wings of the Vulcan, I thought it would have made an ideal shearing shed. Expensive but waterproof. In one of the planes, a Fairey Rotodyne—a machine capable of vertical takeoff—a man dressed in white approached me and began pointing out its special features. He finished his talk by asking if I wanted to buy one.

It was after a banquet of a meal, with one of the companies involved, that the flying itself began. It proved well worth the effort of getting up in the fog at Bristol. The sun was out, making the atmosphere very muggy. During the screaming of jets, which lasted for hours, I began to yearn again for the quietness of the bush. In one pavilion, a display of aeroplane propellers was in the care of General Sir John Evetts. We had quite a long talk about my visit to Redford Barracks in Scotland. He had already been told about most of the happenings, especially the cocoa.

Passing by another display, I was surprised to hear a loud voice calling me by name. I found it belonged to the man in charge of the exhibit, who was named Buckley. The last I had seen of him was in Woomera, driving a car about the village with a large sign on its side which read: *Vote for Buckley*.

Standing alongside a helicopter, I heard a soft voice behind me. Upon turning around I saw my Aldermaston friend Frank Hill, who had remembered that I'd be at Farnborough on the 9th of September. I asked him how he had found me, and he grinned as he explained that he only had to shut his eyes and listen—and come over to where he heard my laugh. After the Show he invited me back for a farewell visit to his house at Mortimer. I couldn't help thinking how wonderful everyone was to me in England. As I only had a week left in the UK before my plane left for Paris, I drove from Frank's place to Brighton the following day. I travelled along the coastline to camp in a private hotel at Hastings near Bexhill. It had been arranged that I pay a last visit to Dover, to see Bob and Betty Genn, with whom I had stayed ten weeks before. I drove through Hastings from where I had originally hired the car. I repeated my former trip to Dover without stopping. On the way I was to carry my last hitchhiking passenger, a Swiss girl named Rosemarie. I wondered if any boys ever hitchhiked.

After three days of alternately baby sitting, drawing pictures of Scottish sheep and touring, I left for Hastings to return the Vauxhall, with only three days left to go. When I drove into the garage nobody there had ever seen me or the car before, but I insisted that they owned it and asked how much I owed them. The speedo indicated that I had driven 5,000 miles, so one of the mechanics rang the owner of the garage. He soon arrived and when I finally convinced him it was his car, I paid him, and he drove me to St Leonards-on-Sea where I could catch a train for London. I was rather sorry to see the car being driven away, as I carried my 'Igh 'Ob'n bag onto the platform.

In London I contacted Jimmy at his office once more, and spent the day waiting until he was to leave for Northwood. I looked at such things as the front door of No.10 Downing Street and the baby called Eros standing on one leg on a pedestal in Piccadilly Circus. Later I collected my permit for Kenya. As I noticed Regent Street near the 'Circus,' with its one-way stream of traffic coming at me, I remembered how I had tried to drive into it with the Vauxhall. A policeman had come rushing over when he saw my radiator face to face with the radiator of a London bus. I remembered how I had explained to him I hadn't the time to talk for long, and asked instead if he would help me sort out the mess. He also guessed I came from Australia.

Throughout the day I remembered to keep well away from The Strand.

On my map I noticed a paddock at the end of Oxford Street, with a creek running through it. So to get away from the angular dust and bus fumes, I made for it. The fumes were already making my eyes red-rimmed. Hyde Park, as it was called, was a welcome change. There was a noticeable absence of peat and heather.

After collecting some boxes of slides in Kingsway, which I had sent off for processing during the trip, I found it was time to join Jimmy and we drove back to Northwood. It was good to see a Londoner driving in the traffic for a change. I told him I was glad it was him at the wheel instead of me.

That night we had a screening of the new set of slides. We all had a pleasant time looking at them. I pointed out that the ones I had taken of Harrison's chronometers in the marine museum at Greenwich did not appear to have come out very well. Jimmy told me that it just so happened he had to go out that way the following day on business, and he could take me along. I suspected he was showing his British hospitality, but was glad of the chance. Many surveyors in Australia would like to see photos of the chronometers.

The day before I left for Paris was, therefore, occupied in taking slides of the famous clocks. I added another picture of the countless already taken of the Tower of London from Tower Bridge. The scene reminded me of an answer to an examination question given by a small boy in Australia when he stated: 'The Tower of London is surrounded by four *peers*, each of which is unfortunately cracked.'

Being in the mood for astronomical observations, after the Greenwich trip, we found there was time enough for Jimmy's sons, Andy and Peter, and myself to visit the planetarium before Jimmy finished at his office. I informed the man in charge of the lecture that I often relied on such observations in Australia to find my way about the desert. We had an interesting chat about it all. He finished by confiding in me that he had never met a real aboriginal before.

Feeling quite sad that this was to be my last day in England, we eventually returned to Northwood. Jimmy went over some details of the trip ahead of me.

I was armed with a fresh book of airline tickets, visas, inoculations, permits and itinerary—mostly arranged by Jimmy—to whom I was so indebted. He and Kay had been wonderful to me and I often marvelled at the chance meeting in London which had led to it all.

After reluctantly saying goodbye to Kay the following morning and loading the 'Igh 'Ob'n' bag into the car, Jimmy drove the children and me to London Airport. Promising to contact several of his special friends for him in Adelaide on my return, I was soon rushed off in the airport bus to the passenger gate, the bag already checked-in at the desk.

I had a last fleeting glance of my friends waving from the rail, and it seemed no time before I was strapping myself into the Air France plane bound for Paris.

Chapter 13

THEN EIFFEL IN SEINE

THE distance from London to Paris is the same as from Adelaide to Port Augusta, so it was only a matter of minutes before we were circling over La Tour Eiffel. A large creek ran past, which, according to the map, I found was named La Seine. Although some paddocks were scattered about, the rest of the ground was covered with a maze of buildings. I couldn't see an ordinary house in any direction to the horizon. Where did everyone live? One paddock, shown as the Bois de Boulogne, looked to be a good camping area, but it would mean a bit of a hike to the creek with a billy for water.

We landed at the airstrip and my trouble started immediately. I couldn't read the French signs, papers, or desk labels. The voice blaring out of a loudspeaker spoke double Dutch to me. The money I had didn't mean anything here at all, but I could see a girl at a counter exchanging some with the passengers. I gave her a handful of sterling notes. She gave me ten handfuls of money in return, which didn't seem so bad.

I wondered where I would start looking for my 'Igh' 'Ob'n bag, and how it would be possible to get to the place the airline had booked me into. Everyone was rushing about like white ants eating plywood. One man I noticed was pacing up and down, watch in one hand, and an irritable look on his face. He was muttering like fury to himself as he went. He paced so fast before turning to retrace his steps that once I thought he wouldn't make it; I imagined him plunging headlong through the glass wall of the air terminal.

My bag was one of a heap near a door marked *Sortie*, so I grabbed it and wondered how I could get out of this building. The name on my list indicated *Hôtel d'Iéna*. I showed it to the uniformed attendant, who was wearing a hat rather like an ice-cream man. He raced past and pointed to some cars outside the *Sortie* door. Complete with my bag and bulging pockets of money, I showed the name to a taxi driver. He bundled me in, slammed the door, and was off to the tune of a squeal of protesting rubber, with me pressed hard into the back of the seat. It was like a blast-off into orbit.

The smell of burnt rubber and brake linings was still with me as I was catapulted out into the footpath. After issuing him with a ladle full of coins from my pocket, he was off as if I had suddenly become radioactive. Maybe he knew something so I resolved to take a bath once installed. At the desk in the lobby the clerk found my name in his book and snapped his fingers, where upon I was immediately set upon by half a dozen bellhops. One snatched my bag, the other pushed a bell for the elevator, another collected a key for my *chambre*. The rest fussed about until we arrived at the room where their main work really began. This consisted of folding back the bed covers, opening windows and all the rest of the heavy slogging which would be too much for their visitor. As soon as each had received a teaspoonful from my pocket, I found I was alone in the room in the space of a heartbeat. I reckoned the one who had opened my bag to lay out my spare shirt earned his tip the most: I accidentally trod on his toe with my desert boots.

I was eager to get to this Eiffel Tower I'd heard about, but decided to have the bath first. I changed into my khaki shorts as it was a hot, muggy morning. Failing to see any water or towel in the room—apart from a small white sink—I picked up the telephone without thinking, only to receive a string of French rattled off like a machine-gun. I mumbled half to myself that it didn't matter, which immediately brought forth some English, enquiring what I had wanted. I told the bloke I was thinking of having a bath, but couldn't find any water. He asked me to wait, calling me *monsieur*. He would arrange it all, and it would also be 500 francs more on my bill. Shortly I heard a knock on the door and casually opened it.

Six ladies were standing there, the leading one carrying a huge key ring like Gabriel, the next in line had an armful of towels, followed by another with a huge lump of soap. Another carried a bottle of stones leaving the last two with a bottle of green water and a pink box of cement. It looked like a line of Zulus reporting for a safari. I'd already worked it out on my cardboard slide rule that this was only going to cost a few bob anyway, but I was getting a little bit nervous as I had heard many stories about Paris. I told them thanks very much, but I didn't have my wheelbarrow with me to get all this stuff to the bathroom, and asked where it was anyway. Something sounding like an aboriginal corroboree followed. Gabriel beckoned me to accompany them, and off we went down the hall with me running to keep up.

There was a small niche in the wall along the corridor into which Gabby plunged, I deduced I was also to enter the room but, when I saw it contained a large bathtub, I began to panic. Everyone was issuing orders, in French, as an enormous tap was thrown open. Hot water gushed out like an artesian bore. The towels were laid out on a marble bench alongside the box of cement. The contents of the green bottle were being emptied into the surging water, and the lump of soap was placed in a wire rack. Just as I wondered about the bottle of stones, the lady opened it and shovelled them into the water as well. I thought it was going to be unnecessarily heavy going, sitting on them during the wash.

Deciding that this was to be my one and only bath in Paris, the tap was turned off, and I looked around pleadingly at the sea of giggling faces about me. To my relief they trooped out leaving me to sit on the stones in comfort.

Bathtime.

B EFORE heading off for the Tower—the top of which I could see from my *chambre* window—I thoughtfully took my *Plan Monumental, avec les compliments de l'Hôtel d'Iéna* with me, in order that the desk clerk could mark an ink cross on the place where I lived, so I could find my way home later. I thought if I could show that to a member of the *Sûreté*, then he could direct me back to the hotel.

As I walked across the lobby in my khaki shorts, watch pouch and desert boots, several very audible gasps came from onlookers, causing me to wonder what was wrong. Maybe it was because I wasn't wearing a tie. The clerk put the required cross on the map, which showed me that the hotel was on the street of the same name, the Avénue d'Iéna. This street seemed to reach a structure resembling an open carport called the *Arc de Triomphe*.

Turning south out of the front door, I excitedly hurried towards the Eiffel Tower, and was soon crossing the bridge which led to *La Tour.* The first aim, of course, was to somehow reach the top. I stood on the road and looked up at this amazing masterpiece in steel. The problem was solved in a remarkably simple way by a sign on one of the legs, through which a lift obviously travelled. It depicted a simple line drawing of the tower with three horizontal arrows pointing at it. The lower one, which was aimed at the lower level, was labelled 100 francs, the middle one pointing to the second floor level read 200 francs, and 500 francs was printed alongside the one aimed at the point on top. I paid the 500 francs thinking it would be easier than climbing the way I did on windpump towers. I then entered into the diamond-shaped box when it came down. Changing boxes on the way, the last one took us up past the soaring vultures, as the framework progressively closed in on us tapering off. This dizzy height was causing me to have second thoughts about all this.

Seeing Paris spread out underneath was really an experience. After several photographs, and the purchase of some postcards for Australia, I lent out over the rail. I wanted to take a view of the tower looking straight down one of its legs. The Citroëns looked like frogs. I thought of this scene when I read in a news article six months later that a woman had jumped over that same rail. As the tower widened towards its base, she would have hit it first on the way down. I had wondered just how they knew it had been a woman.

On the ground again, I reversed the picture to one looking up as I had done with the Empire State Building, when I saw two policemen in ice-cream hats walking towards, me each carrying a sub machine-gun. I quickly got up from the footpath where I was lying and was relieved to see that they strolled right past me. At the stall underneath the tower, I discovered that the price of the postcards rose in proportion to the level from which they were bought. Walking towards the bridge I couldn't help but notice a commotion. I found a traffic policeman yelling at a ragged beggar in the roadway, who was dragging an old pram full of rags and rubbish with a rope while a second pram trailed in tow. Obviously the officer wished the beggar would transfer his pram train off the busy road to the sidewalk, but the beggar, screeching at the top of his voice, seemed quite unwilling. Suddenly—leaving the traffic to the mercy of blaring horns—the gendarme raced over, to the cheers from a bunch of enthusiastic onlookers and grabbed the leading pram, throwing it bodily into the sidewalk. The one in tow went too, but not before it had knocked him off balance, landing him on the road with his head and shoulders protruding from the spilled contents. The policeman did look rather odd, sitting there almost buried in rags, with his face growing a richer hue of purple by the minute. Extricating himself, he seized the beggar and pushed him on top of the overturned prams, after which he strode back to his place directing the traffic. The beggar levered himself out of the pram in which he had jammed and, screeching to the onlookers, began rummaging through the mess for a large carving fork. From his actions, I gathered his intention was to rush out and prod it into the policeman in a rather painful spot, and his audience screamed with delight. As I was thinking this should be worth watching, somebody managed to convince him that such an act might land him in the Bastille, or some such place, if he persisted and I re-crossed the creek feeling quite disappointed.

A large road, shown on the map running through Paris, had the name Avénue des Champs Elysées printed along it. I made for it, to see some more of the city. It seemed incredible that only several hours before I had been in London. Passing my hotel I drew near the Arc de Triomphe. I found it much more substantial than a carport, and noticed a small campfire alight underneath it. I was told this flame was never allowed to go out, and thought we could do with that at times in the bush. From the top I saw the tree-lined avenues radiating in every direction, with no shop awnings over the sidewalks, apart from coloured canvas tent flys. A photo later and I was descending to walk along the Champs Elysées. I was feeling hungry by now, but there didn't appear to be anywhere I could have something to eat, except at the occasional groups of tables arrayed under the hot sun in the gutter, where people were sitting. I had had enough of that in my own camps, so I temporarily gave up the idea of eating.

The cars were screaming around corners on two wheels all about me, with horns blaring. Over the general noise I kept hearing something like the yodelling of a Swiss mountaineer. There was no-one to ask, so I accepted it until I later saw a van full of people from Interpol careering along, with all the corners jutting out into the wind and emitting this same yodelling. I gathered this particular noise took the place of police and fire engine sirens.

As I was standing next to a tall, thin piece of rock balancing upright at one spot called the Place de la Concorde, a light aircraft sky-writing above spelled out an advertisement for some café or other. After the pilot had written it in white smoke, I wondered idly if he would add the little extra bit over the 'e' in café as I had seen it written in Australia. Sure enough, as I watched I saw him climb, turn and dive towards the letter, letting out a little puff in just the right place.

It was well after dark when I started back to my hotel, hungry as ever, but this feeling suddenly vanished when a young lady— who was a complete stranger to me—stopped me and said 'Bonsoir.' I thought she had said 'bonfire' so I asked her 'where?' but this seemed quite the wrong thing to say. She slipped into English and repeated 'Good Evening.' I replied that it certainly was nice, and walked on thinking how friendly the people here were.

Everyone seemed to be constantly staring at me, but I put it down to my imagination, until I hit on an idea. Pushing my woollen socks down around my ankles—half covering the desert boots—I found from then on I barely received a second glance.

The following morning, after leaving my passport tucked into a torn flap in the floral wallpaper in my room, I went down to have some breakfast, remembering the last time I had eaten was at Northwood. The waiter and I couldn't understand each other, so I solved this by taking out a pencil and sketching the things I required on one of the paper napkins. I drew a pig indicating some bacon, and a chook sitting on some eggs to go with it. The waiter went off, napkin and all, laughing at the top of his voice, and showed it to the others on the way to the cook. It might have seemed a joke to him, but to me it was a matter of life or death from malnutrition. He returned with some bacon and eggs, but the mug of tea which I drew proved too much for him, so I settled for water, drawing a large tap and glass. He came back with a bottle of mineral water, which tasted worse than that which we obtained from many of the bores we had sunk back in the bush.

I had arranged for a bus trip around Paris and a vehicle arrived at the hotel door at the appointed time. It was to cost me 1,000 francs, or twice the price of a bath.

At Notre Dame, I hurried through the door—thinking of all that molten lead the bloke on top poured over everyone. The time allotted for passengers at the Louvre was used up in an unsuccessful attempt to see the Mona Lisa. The front door had a man guarding it with a book of tickets, one of which I bought. Inside, a second man sold me another to enter a little further. At a junction of the corridors another ticket-holder waited to sell a pass, to go one way or the other. I wondered where this was going to end. Time was running out, so I did the same, thinking as I went that there was no wonder Lisa was a Moaner.

At the end of the tour I took to hiking again. I wanted to examine an area I had heard about called Pigalle. I decided to catch an underground train. I asked a policeman where I could get a train, but he scowled something at me in French, and continued on directing the traffic with the wooden club he had in his hand. I noticed a hole in the footpath with steps leading down over which a large sign read *Metro*, so I tentatively tried these. I soon found that they led down to the railway and not as I thought, to a cinema. I said the word 'Pigalle' to a man behind bars at a window and he threw a ticket at me, snatching what money he wanted for it out of my hand.

A train shot out from the black hole at the end of the platform and screamed to a halt with its automatic doors opening in the one action. I was able to just scramble in before the doors snapped shut again, almost chopping my elbow off and we were hurtling through the tube a second later. The passengers were all bundled together like bunches of tent pegs, the heap being re-arranged at each stop. Finally the word Pigalle appeared on one platform, and it was only by loosening some of the pegs that I was able to leap out in time before the train vanished again. I walked along a tunnel expecting to see some stairs which would allow me to surface, but arrived instead at a fork. They both were clearly signposted, but the signs meant nothing to me. One said *Sortie* and as I didn't want to go to *Sortie* I tried the other. This lead to yet another fork, but neither sign said Pigalle. I proceeded along one of them to another junction. After having survived the Gibson Desert in Australia I now began to have visions of perishing underground in this miserable Paris rabbit warren. At this stage I suddenly remembered the doorway at the airport. It had been labelled *Sortie* and it had also lead out into the open. Back tracking to the first fork, I took the Sortie tunnel and soon was climbing stairs, which took me back to the surface of the earth. I had learned a French word on my own. The 'Bonsoir' one had been taught to me by the friendly lady.

It was almost dark, so I checked my position by counting the numbers of letters on the street signs, and comparing it with the number of letters on the map. As I walked along one lane it suddenly turned quite dark and I looked up to see a giant of a man shuffling towards me. His shoulders scraped both sides of the unlit alley as he swayed with his arms hanging down to his knees. I thought of my passport tucked safely into the flap of the wallpaper. He got closer with his black sunglasses covering most of his upper face. Edging past him, I continued, only to hear him padding surprisingly softly behind me, having turned to follow. I thought of how he could have driven me down through the cobbles with one swipe of his paw, so instead of threatening him, I turned and walked back to pass him once more. This interesting manoeuvre confused him. I noticed his hairy arms swinging aimlessly and his huge jaw sagging wide open, putting me in mind of a bewildered ape. Not that I'd ever seen a bewildered ape.

This new course led me past an establishment called the *Folies Bergères* and the name rang a bell. From the photographs of the entertainers pasted outside I hoped for their sakes it was not too cold inside. I couldn't find out, dressed as I was in desert boots and shorts. Eventually with the help of my map I arrived at Pigalle, the proof of which was given by the sign Boulevard de Clichy which agreed with the one on the plan. They must have used bore water because the first thing I noticed was a windmill painted with rustproof red lead. I decided first to obtain a prolonged exposure photograph of this place, while resting the camera on the roof of a parked Citroën. Looking around, I saw a crowd gathering and wondered what was wrong, until I realised that their attention was not centred on me at all, but to something inside the Citroën. When I made a grab for my watch pouch to see the time, they dispersed as if by magic, probably taking me for a quick-draw Texan. One stayed, however, and tried to sell me some postcards, but I explained I had already got some from the top of the Eiffel Tower. His were, however, of somewhat different subjects.

The windmill didn't seem to be working properly, so I deduced they must have pumped enough water already. When I got to it, I noticed some other pictures of lady entertainers wearing chilly-looking costumes under a large sign which read *Moulin Rouge*.

Just past this place another narrow, dimly-lit alley went off to the right. I was surprised to see that each doorway was closely guarded. As the guards were all girls, this led me to believe the contents of the buildings couldn't be very valuable after all. They would probably help each other in the event of a break-in by an intruder, but some of the men idly sitting around the tables on the footpaths should have been recruited for the job.

Overhead, an enormous neon sign brightly advertised socks. I couldn't understand the words, but I must have been right as they were the only item worn by the lady outlined in the coloured tubing. I saw something about a French Can-Can at the mill. It made me think of our Australian Wagga-Wagga.

I didn't have a clue as to where I was in relationship to the ink cross on my map. It was about nine o'clock and very late to be up. I decided to hike home, not wanting to get mixed up in the *Sortie* tunnels again so soon.

Scaling the bearing and distance off the map I looked up at the sky, relieved to see some stars, from which I could find north. This enabled me to head off from Pigalle in a south-westerly direction. At one point where the avenues, boulevards, rues and streets went off in every direction, like a spider web without the transoms, I paused to consult the stars and map again. Another friendly lady approached me to say 'Bonsoir.' After endeavouring to say the same thing, my accent caused her to repeat it in English. I thought how easily she could find a job as an interpreter. She seemed to be a bit lost, and she asked me if I could see her to where she lived, but I explained that I didn't live in Paris and was having some trouble myself. Nevertheless I offered to give her my map which might help her. I could rely on the stars to guide me back, and consoled her by telling her I could understand her anxiety at being out at this time of night on her own. It was past 10.30 already.

With that, she turned and clattered off down the cobbled alley, her stiletto heels sending sparks off the stones. Perhaps she hadn't heard of anyone finding their way about by the stars before.

As I cut my previous tracks on the Champs Elysées, I could hear the yodelling of the police cars, the squealing of tyres and see a blur of vehicles rocketing along four abreast. I wondered where they were all off to. It took me twenty minutes to gain the courage necessary to make the charge across the road opposite the *Lido* sign, after which I found the Arc de Triomphe, turned south and was soon in my hotel *chambre*. Being weak from hunger, the next morning I decided to have some sausages. I drew a picture of an irate butcher wielding a meat cleaver and chasing a dog running out of his shop with a string of sausages in his mouth. I circled four sausages at the end of the string—to ensure I didn't get baked dog instead—I gave the napkin to a white-coated waiter who went off to the kitchen, where it was pinned to the wall on my private art gallery, amid much excited laughing.

While waiting to travel to the air terminal, as I was due off again that morning, I went to see some more of the surroundings of the tower. One grass plot near some gardens was ringed by an iron fence. Here I saw a very substantial-looking woman, through the upright bars, busily moving a great pile of rags from one corner to the other. She was about sixty years of age, with her mouth outlined in thick scarlet lipstick, under big bright red patches on each cheek made with coloured ochre. I watched as she worked like a slave until all the rags were in a bundle in a second corner of the cage. I wondered what all these people did with their rags, thinking of the load on the pram train. Without losing a second, she promptly began to transport them all back to their original corner. She was far from *petite*; the rivers of perspiration caused the ochre to streak down her face in ever-increasing watercourses. I carried on after watching her repeat this performance half-a-dozen times, thinking there was no particular reason why she should not move rags about all day if she felt like it.

As I ambled back another woman came past me at full gallop out of a shop and to her car. She leapt in and took off like a bullet the moment the door slammed shut. She turned a corner ten yards away—on two wheels. Several yards further she slammed on the brakes again, charging out, and into another shop door to continue with her purchases. She had driven the 30 yards at break-neck speed, in three seconds. A little further on I saw a lady approaching, carrying a tent pole over her shoulder. As she neared the pole took on an odd appearance. When I was next to her I saw it to be in effect a loaf of bread two inches in diameter and at least five feet long.

On returning to the hotel I couldn't help noticing a man standing in a little sheet-iron cage on the sidewalk holding hands with a young lady. I'd already noticed a similar scene before, and had wondered about it. It could have been that he was sheltering from the wind had there been any, but in that case his hat would not have still been on. This was certainly a strange place.

Extricating my passport from the flap, settling my account for 9,500 francs with another 300 for the taxi to the air terminal and 700 more for the bus to the airport, I eventually found myself waiting for the Swissair plane to Zurich. I changed my remaining French francs into Swiss francs, but as these were of a vastly different value, my pockets of money dwindled to the few equivalent coins. We circled over Paris before heading off. I heard a soft voice at my elbow purring 'Bonjour.' I thought to myself: 'Oh no, here we go again.' At least I know what *Sortie* means.

Chapter 14

THE PRECISION COUNTRY

JUST an hour and a quarter later, we were taxiing along a runway at Zurich airport. The change in general tempo and atmosphere was immediately apparent. There were open paddocks everywhere and only a handful of people. It was incredible that there was such a marked difference in so short a distance. It was right there and then that the phrase *Around the World in Eighty Delays* occurred to me.

During the flight I had studied the pamphlet tucked in the pocket of the aircraft seat. It was entitled 'How to get along with the Swiss' and one story, which was obviously a good-humoured dig at themselves, kept revolving in my mind. It was about the first man the Lord had brought to this land. Before he left, he told the man to make three wishes, which would be granted. The delighted newcomer first asked for many high, snow-capped mountains from which he could view his new and wonderful country. He could also be closer to Heaven. The Lord was very pleased at this request, resulting in the sudden appearance of a great number of beautiful peaks all around. On being asked for his second wish, the man asked for a fine herd of cows, from which he could obtain all the fresh milk he wanted, in order that he may be kept strong to climb the peaks. The Lord was equally pleased with this wish. In a flash a herd appeared, grazing on fresh green grass. The man thanked the Lord gratefully and went over immediately to milk one of the cows. He collected the milk in a curved stone, from which he drank deeply, and it was good. As he filled the stone with more milk, the Lord asked him what his third wish was going to be. The man offered the curved stone full of milk to the Lord. He replied that his third wish was that the Lord drank the rich milk therein, as a token of his appreciation. The Lord knew immediately that he had made the right choice of person for this new land and drank the milk. As the Lord returned the vessel to his new subject the man held out his other hand and said 'That will be one franc twenty.'

With this in mind, I changed another traveller's cheque at the airport. I was transported to the terminal, which cost me two francs, and continued on to the Rex Hotel by taxi which was another two.

THE desk clerk found my name on his book and gave me a tremendous pear-shaped lump of solid rubber. I wasn't exactly sure what I was supposed to do with this, until I discovered a small key, where the stalk would normally attach. It was my room key. As I unlocked the door the rubber pear made only a *quiet* thud. When released, it didn't make the clanking of the usual brass tag. There was a bed inside the room, and another installation which looked rather like a tiled incinerator. It was cube-shaped and a few feet across. There was a tap leading in to it, to put the fire out for safety. I hadn't accumulated very much rubbish yet so I wondered at such an unusual addition to a room. There was no bath in the room as the booklet indicated, and it occurred to me the cube must be *it*, which would explain the addition of the tap. After all that hiking around Paris and not having had a bath since the *tub of stones* episode, I tried it out. However, I first sat on the floor to give myself a haircut.

Climbing into the cube, I found I could sit down only with my knees nestled under my ears. The water rose to my armpits soon after turning on the tap. After a while, I tried to get out of this thing, but seemed to be wedged. If it hadn't been for the plastic curtain which I used as a climbing rope, I would have been there for quite a while. Finishing the bath by kneeling on the edge and standing on my head in the water, I redressed and went down to the desk to arrange a trip to the Matterhorn. I also wanted to visit Heerbrugg where there was a factory for precise instruments. Many such instruments I had used, carrying out surveys in Australia. The clerk advised me about bus trips, but this didn't include everything during the time I had available. He rang a car hire firm and handed me the phone. We organised a Volkswagen to be delivered in the morning, to the Hotel Rex. I planned to leave the car at the airport several days later, on my way to the plane.

Walking around Zurich—past a Swiss National Bank which I was told held half of the world's gold bullion—I came to the shopping area of town, with its dozens of watch and jewellery establishments. The windows were loaded with masterpieces of craftsmanship. One particularly elaborate shop held a flexible string of gold, the thickness of number 8 fencing wire, placed upon a velvet pad. In the middle of its length I noticed an almost imperceptible swelling in diameter, such as a snake has after eating a mouse. As I looked I was astounded to see that the whole thing was really a wristwatch, the dial and works were set in the swollen part, with the hands under the glass. A pin head would have covered it completely. On my way back to the hotel—with the rubber pear sagging at my pocket—I unwillingly became a witness to an accident, in which a whole shop front was torn down ever so carefully by a ten-ton truck.

Early in the morning, I was already at the desk when a most pleasant Swiss girl came into the lobby. She spoke to the clerk in German, who replied by pointing in my direction, where I sat waiting next to my 'Igh 'Ob'n bag. She changed to English and asked me to fill in some forms. She assured me my driving licence was recognised here. With that, she asked if I could possibly drop her off at her office, as it was on my way out of Zurich. I told her I'd be only too pleased and we went off to the Volkswagen. I paid my bill as I wouldn't be returning.

It was a left-hand drive vehicle and we drove away with her advising me on some of the traffic rules. She finally indicated her stop, by patting my hand on the gear lever and wishing me a pleasant trip. I decided there and then I would never wash that hand again. I was in Rome before I had the chance.

I passed through Luzern and Gletsch, then along a straight valley scattered with several settlements. The buildings were all made of strong logs. They had to be strong to support the roofs of great slabs of flat stone, which were not only water and hail proof, but also air raid resistant.

In Brig, at the end of the valley, the trip meter had notched up 150 since leaving Zurich. I decided to fill the petrol tank, not being sure if any more would be available for the return trip of 60 miles to the Matterhorn. When I asked for several gallons of petrol, the garage attendant looked at me as if I were from some strange distant land. When I pointed to the fuel cap his face told me he understood. He mentioned something about *litres of essence*. Without asking what flavour he got to work, in no time he was returning the hose to its bowser. It was then I realised I'd come only 150 *kilometres*. It also explained how I'd come to be driving around hairpin bends at breakneck speeds, according to the metric speedo.

I was anxious to carry on to St. Nicklaus, where the road appeared to end. I had to find a place to camp, and discover how I could proceed to Zermatt—from where I could see the famous 15,000-foot Matterhorn. Suddenly I saw a lorry on *his* wrong side of the road coming straight towards me at a great rate. It caused me to drive up on to the footpath and past some shop windows, to avoid a collision. It was only after I noticed a car following that I realised that he'd been on *his* correct side all the time, and I was the one who was wrong. A man came out of a chemist shop to see me. The car had pulled up a foot from his door, so I bought a film from him without getting out and drove back over the gutter to the opposite side of the road. He must have thought me extremely lazy. I saw him through the rear-vision mirror staring after me, scratching his head.

DRIVING to a dead-end in the road, which placed me in the middle of the village square in St. Nicklaus, I climbed out to see the people, sitting silently studying my hunting knife and boots. One weather-beaten ancient I addressed knew nothing of English, but instead directed me to someone else. After eight tries I began to despair, so I took out a pencil and paper. I drew a bed with myself asleep on it, and held it up for general inspection. I'd been advised not to worry about the first impression when talking to a Swiss. They only want to give you the initiative. As their long faces turned to smiles, one man came forward with a long-handled shovel, on which he had been leaning. I thought for a while that he was an Australian, but instead he picked up a piece of white stone and wrote something on the shovel, which he handed to me. He pointed to a building on top of a steep incline. I could only thank him with a smile, and as I climbed the miniature cliff, clutching the shovel, I was glad I was at least making use of my boots. The building, under the shadow of a high jagged mountain, turned out to be a railway station. It seemed an odd sort of hotel, but nevertheless I went into the ticket office, brandishing the shovel. One man read the word on it, and pointed to another, whom I approached with the round-mouthed shovel blade held out in front.

Apparently it had his name written on it. He began to talk to me in English, which caused me extreme pleasure, as I hadn't understood anyone since leaving London. It seemed he was the only one here who knew something of the language, so he explained that a room could be had in a white building bordering the square. Back down the cliff again, I handed the owner back his shovel—to lean on again before he fell right over—and entered the establishment indicated. Soon I was in a room, with the help of some children who lived there. I spent what was left of the day communicating with them by means of drawings on a pad of paper. After each drawing, I would print the English word meaning the item and they would add the Swiss word equivalent. They took it as great fun. By the time we had finished, the pad looked like a cross between a language dictionary and the beginnings of an art course. I had arranged a ticket on a mountain train for the morning, to take me to Zermatt. From there I could board the flying fox car. This would transport me to a plateau which was the nearest I could get to the Matterhorn without hiking.

The train wound through some of the most wonderful country. It was as beautiful as anything in the world. I stopped at Zermatt where there were coloured coaches drawn by white horses whose harness was decorated with brightly-polished brass fittings. They were waiting to take people and their luggage to their hotels.

The coachmen, in their brightly-coloured dress, might have looked a little out of place in a bush mustering camp, but they certainly fitted into this atmosphere perfectly. The buildings still had rock roofs and were constructed of logs. Many overlooked the glacier flowing from the Matterhorn. It could be easily seen, snow-capped and rearing up 15,000 feet into the sky, only a few miles away. It was a scene worth travelling across the world to view. Finding the cable car terminal, I climbed into one and we were soon gliding up the plateau, high above the valley below. Small huts could be seen, with their rocky roofs and cows grazing about. I thought of what a wild ride it would be if the retaining cable came adrift.

Taking a note of the times for the return trip, I began walking towards this most famous of landmarks, taking the occasional photograph. I soon found I was having some difficulty in breathing, and decided that although I was used to climbing mountains, carrying a theodolite on my back for surveys in Australia, I must have become somewhat out of condition on this trip.

The craggy peak was looming higher and higher. As I drew nearer it seemed to be almost over me, such were its massive proportions. A man came walking towards me and told me, in English, that I was walking much too fast in this thin air, and to go much slower. It only then occurred to me that I had been used to denser air and realised how high I was above sea level. I thought of the ones who had conquered it, and how many lives had been lost in trying.

Eventually, arriving at what I thought was near enough to its base, I looked at my belt watch and decided I must start the return walk to the cable way. There was only one more cable car going down today. The view of the surrounding peaks from here was quite breathtaking in more ways than one, I thought, as I gasped for air. I was in a hurry, but could not help comparing it with the Nullarbor Plain from where I had started on this trip.

At the plateau I took a photograph of a particularly striking view showing the glacier, only to see an identical picture on a calendar the following year back in Adelaide.

There was an American couple with me in the cable car on the way down. As they were from Manhattan I told them of my experiences, including the one involving the jeweller and my lack of friends with four ears. They made the whole car shake with their laughing, as they re-enacted the scene in their minds.

I reluctantly found myself on the train returning to St. Nicklaus. Once back I returned to the hotel, after checking that the Volkswagen was all right. I spent another night drawing pictures for a much enlarged group of children.

It took all my willpower to drive away the following morning. I headed back to Brig, where there was a junction of roads, one of which would take me down into Italy. Driving rapidly past the chemist shop, I took the Domodossola road, which climbed immediately into a heavy bank of clouds. I had no doubt the scenery would have been equally as perfect, but as I couldn't see any further than a few yards in front of the car, I wasn't able to make the most of it, much to my loss. Periodically a chomping sound of marching boots could be heard. A squad of uniformed soldiers would materialise out of the fog, to come sloshing past me on the unpaved road. I seemed to be constantly crossing creeks, and wished we could have had the same in the bush.

Suddenly, a guard appeared standing on the road in front of me. He was complete with a machine-gun levelled at a spot roughly between my eyes. It took no further persuasion to convince me to stop and the man came to my window saying the one word 'Passport.' I gently eased the muzzle of the gun away, telling him not to do anything hasty, as I handed my passport over, leaving him to disappear into a hut with it. He came out soon after, handed it back and from an inspection of the rubber stamp placed upon it I gathered this was the Swiss-Italian frontier. I was glad they didn't carry on like this on drives from Adelaide to Alice Springs.

He was soon lost to view in the swirling fog behind me; the last I saw of him made me think that he was quite disappointed in not having been given the chance to squeeze the trigger. At Domodossola a small boy came out on to the road and waved me to stop. As soon as I had, he made a turning gesture with his hands, pointing to an obscure turnoff. He waved me into it as he would a herd of cows. I drove along it obediently, only to see a sign for Locarno, which was where I had planned on going. The boy obviously must have been used to newcomers missing this turn, and helped them as he had me, thus saving us all from driving to Milan by mistake. He assumed that nobody could possibly have wanted to go to Milan.

On the way, after many crossings and re-crossings of creeks, another sub machine-gun bailed me up, and took my passport into the shed. Another rubber stamp, and I was across the border back into Switzerland. I was driving through Locarno at the northern end of a good-sized waterhole. When I arrived at a place with the most unlikely name of Chur, it was dark. Apart from needing something to eat, I was also thinking of camping for the night, so went into a house—armed with pencil and paper—hoping to discover a likely spot. The door opened and to my surprise, it was almost slammed shut again in my face, as the occupants saw me with my pencil poised over the paper. I must have looked like a detective and wondered why they should have had such a guilty conscience, as I returned to the car and hastily drove away.

Soon after that I noticed a well-lit building across a paddock. I went to it and found a man to whom I could show my drawing of a bed with me asleep on it. He immediately burst out laughing.

Leading me into the building and through a door, I saw several carcasses hanging up between blocks of ice lining the walls. It must have been an abattoir, but he took my pencil and wrote the word *bett* under my sketch. This was what I should ask for if ever I wanted a bed in the future.

I felt tired and hungry as I drove off, but carried on until another machine-gun told me it would be better if I stopped. I automatically handed over my passport. When the passport came back out of the shed, with the addition of another rubber stamp, I asked where I could find a *bett*. It sounded to me as if I were looking for a bookmaker, but he impatiently waved me on, with an angry sweep of the machine-gun barrel. I was now in Austria. At this rate I began to hope my passport was going to be large enough for all the rubber stamps.

I couldn't believe my eyes, when I found I was staring down the bore of another machine-gun, yet again out with the passport, and into his shed, back again with another rubber stamp, and off once more into Switzerland. I decided then that I'd go right on into Heerbrugg before camping. I would sleep in the Volkswagen there if I had to.

Arriving at this city, the name of which I had seen for years on so many instruments, I found a hotel. I went in and asked the girls at the desk for a *bett*. From my accent she concluded that that was all the Swiss I knew, so a man came in answer to a button which had been pressed. He arranged it all for me in English, and showed me to my room. It was nearing midnight and I had driven from the Matterhorn that morning, but I was still hungry enough to ask him if I could have something to eat. He left me in a dining room which was still occupied. I went over to an empty table.

While I was eating a couple came in and asked me, in English, whether I'd mind if they sat at my table. I was very pleased to and we soon began talking about the *Wild* instrument factory. He said he worked in the optical department and offered to arrange for a manager to show me around the plant the next morning. After he'd telephoned a Mr Kindler, I thought how lucky I was to have met him. I asked him what everyone did in Heerbrugg. He told me that almost everybody worked at *Wild*.

Being Saturday, the factory was empty. Mr Kindler walked to the hotel and I drove him in the Volkswagen. Every room and laboratory was like an operating theatre, without a speck of dust to be seen anywhere. He took me on a complete tour, explaining things as we went. The difference was that here I couldn't photograph anything, as I had been allowed to back in York. Boxes of theodolites, sets of drawing instruments, levels and precision machines were stacked in readiness for dispatch to all parts of the world. I concluded that it had been well worth all the machine-guns to look over one of the ultimate factories for precision and cleanliness to be found in the world.

After delivering Mr Kindler back to his home, I remembered that my plane left Zurich, a hundred kilometres away, that same afternoon. I was headed for Venice so I set off towards the place shown on my map, with another unlikely name: Wil, via Gallen. Every other place named in the vicinity finished up with *wil*. On seeing one called Wattwil I hurried faster than before, as I thought aloud 'What will I do if I miss the plane' I filled the car with 18 *litres of essence* before taking off.

On this last section of my semi-circumnavigation of Switzerland, I noticed an enormous brass bell held up by a great leather strap, with a shining brass six-inch buckle. Soon after I noticed that it was around a cow's neck. As the unfortunate animal ambled along, it clanged deafeningly, reminding me of my experiences at Big Ben. Further on there was another. After that every cow I saw was wearing one. I gathered the farmers could find their herds easily in the fog with all that noise going on. I saw one paddock the size of a tennis court with a small herd of cows wearing one each. It must have driven the cows mad. One extra-large one—looking more like a school bell—was tended by a boy. I approached him with my camera. The boy held the horns for me. He must have been used to this with each newcomer. I noticed how strong the necks of Swiss cows had to be. It made my own leather belt look like a watch strap in comparison.

I was soon driving into Zurich after the 100 kilometre drive from Heerbrugg. The first people I met were two policemen in a car, both of whom chastised me in sign language when I stopped in the middle of the traffic to consult my map. It must have been very windy, because these were normally a very placid people. I understand that when a certain wind blows in Switzerland anyone can legally murder their mother-in-law.

Driving past several large clean-looking establishments situated on bright green lawns, with the names of several well-known makes of Swiss watches upon them, I followed the signs for something like *Flughafen*. It apparently meant airport. I discovered this after showing somebody a drawing of an aeroplane.

Time was getting on, so I parked the faithful Volkswagen, which hadn't missed a beat after my 700 kilometre trip. Grabbing the 'Igh 'Ob'n bag, and darting into the air terminal buildings, I found a desk with the name of the car hire firm on it. I rushed over and dropped the keys on the clerk's desk. Paying him the equivalent of £19-13-0 as requested, I raced for the Alitalia desk, showed them my book of tickets and checked in the bag. It was here I noticed what slaves the Swiss were to their precision watches. Clocks and watches were everywhere, and small desks were scattered about the airport buildings, each with the firm's name they represented printed on large signs.

As I sat watching people getting last-minute watches, I noticed two doors with the labels *Heifers* and *Steers* marked on them. As I watched, a red-faced lady emerged from *Steers*. Children were doing a brisk trade with large chocolates covered in gold foil, in the shape of Swiss coins, relieving passengers of their centimes which were too small to change into lire. I obtained several with mine.

As I walked past this glittering array of precision timepieces, I thought of the story which showed just what sort of slaves the Swiss were to their watches. It happened that as one speaker sat down after giving a lecture at a meeting in a watch factory, there had been a complete silence before a loud and long burst of cheering and clapping showed the audience's appreciation. When it came to an end one man leaned over to his neighbour and informed him that the applause had lasted for 3 minutes 53.7 seconds.

Chapter 15

THE PETRIFIED PEOPLE

THE 150-mile flight to Milan was made all the way in heavy cloud. The fact that we landed safely on instruments, proved they knew the height of the Swiss Alps over which we flew. They were very likely the same clouds which I drove the Volkswagen through in the machine-gun country which was only 50 miles away.

All flights out of Milan were cancelled as a result of the cloud, so the airline booked the passengers into the Excelsior Hotel at Gallia, which was an hour's bus ride from the airport. I wasn't looking forward to the temperature in the room. The air conditioner maintained it at 23 degrees, a figure I had read in their booklet. As water froze at 32 degrees, I was preparing for a rather brisk evening's sleep, until I discovered it was all in *centigrade*.

In the dining room five waiters descended on my little table. While one unfolded the napkin, another laid out the spoon and fork, while another poured out a mug of water. The fourth arranged some flowers, leaving the last one to actually take the order. I pointed to various items on the menu, hoping they were to be eaten and not played by the two-piece band present. At the end of the meal I pointed to a large iced cake I had been eyeing on another table. A right-angled wedge was cut off and handed over. The other waiters carried away the plates and spoon as soon as I finished with them, because I was the only one left in the room. It rather resembled the service I received when I had the bath in Paris.

Later on, walking around Milan, I saw the most beautifully built church possible, the roof of countless spikes pointing skyward. I idly wondered what would happen to an unlucky parachutist.

Next morning, after the hour's bus ride to the Alitalia Air Terminal, we flew 150 miles east to Venice, and out of the cloud bank. We soon found ourselves travelling on a river bus along the Grand Canal. As I left my 'Igh 'Ob'n bag at the airport, I had only a spare shirt. Once deposited at St. Marco Square and left on my own, I walked to the Hotel Pensione Flora. I was glad to see that my name was on *their* register when I walked into the darkened lobby. The manager directed me to a room.

It seems that once there was a tribe of Barbarians, who were disappointed with their own patch and kept invading others. The Venetians constructed this town on a nest of 118 islands separated by 160 canals, to confuse them. To save themselves having to swim over the canals to see each other, a system of 400 miniature foot bridges was built. The foundations of the buildings were, therefore, not very solidly built: they were on a swamp. Most of the towers had a noticeable lean, but somehow seemed to stay up. One bridge, the Rialto, was covered with shops rising in stages from each bank to the centre. It was rather as if they had been built on the outside curve of a boomerang, standing on edge. Today, along the centre of the covered footpath between the shops were stalls selling sunglasses. I met a visiting German on this bridge, on holiday away from his wife, he told me in broken English. His eyes sparkled as he went on to inform me that his wife had allowed him an annual release. She told him that if he met a pretty girl on his trip then it would be all right if he 'kissed she.'

Everyone wanted to take me for a ride on a gondola. I told one persistent boatman that I had forgotten to bring my sextant. His mouth fell open and he scratched his head. This allowed me to creep away, as he endeavoured to work that one out. The operator pushes the craft along with a post he carries for the purpose. I observed a wedding, where the couple came out of the church to step into a specially-appointed black gondola, with the post-pusher dressed in dazzling white. He took them to a waiting ship at the head of the Adriatic.

While walking along the line of shops near St. Marco Square, I became aware of a shadowy figure following me. I noticed it was wearing heavy sunglasses. Every time I stopped to look into a window the figure did the same. This went on for a quarter of an hour. He trailed noiselessly behind me. Everywhere I led he followed like a faithful St. Bernard dog. Half an hour later I turned in my tracks and stood in front of him, asking him if he had a compass of his own. He stared at me for a minute without talking, turned on his heel and shuffled away. He must have had one after all.

On one boat excursion, to see the glass-blowers on Murano island, I met a couple by the name of Graham and June Ward. They told me they were visiting from Nairobi. As soon as I mentioned I'd be there in a week myself, they insisted I contact them upon arrival and would show me the main sights. On Murano, all the men working the glass had cheeks like balloons. They blew the glass into every conceivable shape. We moved to another island, Burano, where they were busy doing their best to make the Venetians blind. It was in a dull, unlit room where rows of girls sat straining their eyes over yards of fine lace.

Back in Venice, I went to see the Bridge of Sighs, over which convicts used to be sent to their dank little dungeons, never to return. I crawled into one of them, but hurried out in case somebody happened to slam the heavy iron door. The criminals, without exception, lost interest in everything once they had made the trip over the bridge. They probably welcomed the rats, which came to chew them to death. One canal was being cleaned, but as I couldn't hold my breath for more than a minute, I had to leave the two men in the ditch on their own. They worked with shovels, up to their knees in mud, and seemed quite oblivious to the aroma. One of the oddest features of this place were the breakfasts, consisting of bread horseshoes and apricot jam, with a mug of gun powder and water for coffee. I repeatedly drew sketches of bacon and eggs, but the drawings fell on blind eyes.

At St. Marco Square, a man on top of a building would come out periodically with a sledge hammer and beat a gong, marking the hour. I was quite relieved for his sake to discover he was only a mechanical model. After walking up the concrete ramps inside the tower on the square, to obtain some pictures of the town, I became so hungry that I bought some bread and cheese. I sat on the wall of a water street to eat them, watching the stream of trash as it floated past. I was almost starving by the time the river bus was ready to take me back to the *aeroporto* a day later. After another breakfast of bread horseshoes I was airborne. I was glad to have seen this amazing place from the air, with its barbers' poles growing out of the streets at every doorway. The hostess on the aeroplane told me they were hitching posts for boats. We were off to Florence, 150 miles to the south-west. It struck me that everything since leaving Zurich was 150 miles apart.

The hotel in Florence, where I finished up after landing, had my name already in their register. The manager himself offered to show me to my room, about six floors up. After some jabbing at the button, an iron-cage elevator appeared behind a grille. I started to walk in, only to bury myself in the door which failed to open. The manager apologised, and levered open a catch with the bread knife he was carrying. We both struggled with it until there was enough room to squeeze through. We forced it shut, after which he pushed another button as I braced myself for the lift-off. Nothing happened, so he banged the control switch with his fist and pressed the button, sending us skyward. It stopped between floors on the way. By using the handle of the bread knife, he succeeded in tapping the rear of the box, which got us under way once more. It eventually stopped at the floor where my room was located and we levered open the door enough to crawl through. I succeeded in cracking my shins on the floor. The cage had jammed a foot short and this sent me sprawling on my face into the corridor. I struggled up and took my bag from the manager, who helped to force it through the crack. He climbed out of the cage to join me. I helped him to lever his substantial stomach through the opening, before we carried on to the room.

I noticed he had no keys, but on stopping outside the door he tapped the blade of the knife through the slit alongside the lock with the palm of his hand, sending the door open in the action. It only opened three inches, and he forced it the rest with his shoulder against it, apologising all the time. It seemed a little dark inside, so I went to turn on the light, only to be tackled by him around my knees. He explained he had probably saved my life. I should never touch that switch because it sometimes throws you over. I thanked him, and went to open the window. At first it would not budge, but just as I strained it open to let all the fresh gasoline fumes in, the catch tore off in my fingers. I tried the wardrobe door, and this opened *too* easily. The whole thing came away in my hand and fell on top of the manager. Helping him out from under the wardrobe, I told him I was really dreadfully sorry and asked him about the toilet. This meant rolling up my sleeve, removing the cover off the cistern, and feeling about in the water for a copper wire loop. When located, the loop was hooked over the end of a lever. Once used the loop fell off and you had to repeat the performance all over again the next time.

He then told me there was something I should know about the front door. We went out to the elevator, but as the cage refused to come after a quarter of an hour button-jabbing, I told him I would enjoy the walk down the 14 flights of stairs. At the front door he handed me the key, advising me I could let myself in. The key had to be used to lock the door on the way out as well. I did this all right, while he watched, but the key wouldn't come out of the lock. He explained how it was done, as it was a bit tricky unless you knew how. You were required to exert an *extracting* action on the key with one hand, while with the other you needed to press on the inner circle with your thumbnail. A sharp kick at the base of the door would dislodge the key. When I did it, I finished up on the broad of my back on the footpath, but I at least had the key. He spent most of his time apologising, showing me what a very polite man he really was, and ever so helpful with his unique hotel.

With that, I went off with the key to look around. A major feature of this town are the statues, which made some of the village squares look more like stone nudist colonies. They were carved into every conceivable attitude; mostly they were depicting people bashing each other. Some held hatchets, poised to bury the blades into their colleagues white stone heads. Others fought with daggers, leaving a group merely breaking one another's necks with their bare hands. I wondered why the sculptors hadn't used a more genial theme for their work instead of all this violence, but decided people just may have been unhappy in those days.

An American lady asked me if I could photograph her next to one huge white stone character standing on a pedestal, clad only in volumes of stone hair. The rest of him looked as if he could do with a good wash, as his bare shoulders had, for centuries, made ideal perches.

One building complete with a tower and bordering the square of the chilly stone men, housed a painting of a battle scene which was perfect in every detail. It was the most enormous hand-painted picture in the world. I'm sure the artist must have had to ride backwards and forwards along it on horseback as he worked. Even then, he would have needed a bag of chaff to maintain the horse on the way.

Crossing over a creek in the town, the *Fiume Arno*, I climbed up onto some buildings on a hill to the south, to secure a picture of *Firenze* as it was shown on some maps. I finished up on an iron catwalk. This overlooked another statue of Michelangelo, but the walkway was blocked off by a spiked iron fence. As I needed to go further round for the photograph, I climbed over the rail. I manoeuvred along the outside of the rail with my camera looped into my belt. I had a long drop underneath me, but I managed to inch my way around the row of spikes to the other side. I then attempted to re-climb the railings. This proved a little more awkward than I had imagined, but once near the top I fell over onto the iron floor. In the process I brought my knee down heavily on the corner of an iron chair, and lay in agony for a long time, hoping I'd be able to walk again. It was all better in an hour, apart from a gash in the middle of a black bruise, so I took the picture and carried on.

Back across the creek where another street was lined with shops, I walked for as long as I could before gaining courage enough to return to that hotel.

Once inside, I leapt up the 14 flights of stairs to my room. Retrieving the bread knife from our hiding place, I was soon inside feeling more like a member of the Mafia. I decided to take a bath. When I located the plug, I found it wouldn't stay in the hole long enough to keep the water in the tub, so I screwed up a wad of paper and jammed it into the outlet. When I turned on the cold tap the water which gushed out *was* almost boiling hot. After trying the hot tap, I discovered it was actually boiling. By then the cold tap was giving out the same, so I decided to run an aqueduct from the basin, but this water was also boiling. Leaving some water in the tub, I splashed it about with the bread knife until it cooled enough to use, and climbed in. At that moment the level of the water, instead of rising, went down, and I discovered that the paper plug had dissolved. I gave up the idea of a bath and turned to clean my teeth. The water melted the end off my toothbrush, as it sagged down when the water hit it. I went back to the room and took off my desert boots.

As I sat on the bed to take off my socks, one leg of the bed buckled, leaving me to slide, with the mattress, down to the floor. I found I could prop up the bed with a kettle which I found underneath. I then dragged the mattress back into place. All this was done in semi-darkness. I didn't dare touch the switch, but found a dull glow coming in through the window from a neon sign. The sign outside the bathroom window had been much brighter.

After bread horseshoes and apricot jam in the morning, with gunpowder and water solvent, I went to catch the bus, which I had learned would take me to Pisa for the day, providing I gave them enough lire. Being only 40 miles from the Leaning Tower, I had to make the visit.

A S we dropped down into Pisa from a hill, everyone was craning their necks in vain to be the first to see the tower, but it wasn't until we stopped that it became evident. A man came over and explained that 'everyone-a come-a to-a Pisa to see-a the leaning-a tower,' but he impressed upon us the main item of interest should be the church. The leaning tower was merely a belfrey. Nevertheless, all eyes were glued to the famous landmark, as he hurried us into the church which was really more impressive than the tower. It was a work of art in every respect, with its solid-gold leaf panels, but all minds were unwaveringly still fixed on the tower outside, to which he finally allowed us to go. It was remarkable how it could remain standing with such a lean. The structure was said to be slowly moving. It already had a lean of 8 degrees, which meant a 14-foot displacement of the plumb-line. I had often carried out surveys for aligning vertical masts and towers, so I went to a point in the direction of the maximum tilt. I searched for a survey mark on the ground, which would be necessary to measure the rate of movement, and found it was difficult to keep my mind on the search, being so directly under the tower leaning overhead. Sure enough, I came to a brass plate set on a permanent immovable footing. Unfortunately another great hinged brass plate held in place by a heavy brass padlock was over the ground mark, but by lifting this cover a fraction and reflecting sunlight in to the crack with the back of my belt watch, I could see a series of finely scribed lines. These would have been plumbed accurately from some mark set into the top of the tower. By the use of a theodolite, the furthest scratch representing the latest of the readings. Although it had been there for some time I still had the feeling I was glad I didn't live in a house in its path. I could visualise an insurance salesman stating: '…and furthermore, this policy gives you complete coverage against towers dropping on your house.'

Then came the climb up to the top, so I went in through the door at the base, which was sunk in a miniature waterless moat. Inside was a table inclined at a great angle. I wondered why all the pens and ink didn't slide off into the floor, but I realised the table was level and the floor was inclined. It was like being inside a crazy building at Coney Island.

'Gee...sorry.'

The climb up the spiral stairway was equally as disturbing, trying to keep upright with the walls going at right angles as each circuit was completed. The surface of the steps against the inner wall on the uphill side were worn deeply, leaving the outer surface unmarked. When a semi-circle was completed, the reverse was the case, with the stairs worn against the outer wall.

Halfway round they were worn in the middle, but the walls on either side leaned forward—or to the rear—depending upon which side of the tower you were facing. There were openings to the outside pathways encircling the tower at each floor. At your own risk, you could emerge from the steps for a better view.

The tower was begun upright, from all accounts. It remained so until the third storey. One morning the workers found the whole thing leaning: the foundation on one side had subsided. The designer gave up the whole project on the spot. He left it until someone came along and decided to finish it at the same angle. The last section at the top, to take the bell, had an attempt made on it to correct the lean. The new architect thought it could be the last straw: the bell might not swing freely.

Creeping about the top level, I went to the uphill side to see the full length of tower under me, but as I cautiously eased around to the lower side, I could see nothing whatever under me at all. Although it had been there for a long time, I had the feeling that I might just be unlucky enough to be the one to topple it completely. Without its leaning tower the people of Pisa would have been extremely sad.

It is moving very gradually each year, and according to one theory, the collapse could take place during the next century. Experts from all over the world have been wrestling with the problem of stabilising the structure. This could be achieved with support by reinforced concrete. It could be placed under the lower side, allowing the tower to remain static, but still preserving its famous lean.

If such a situation had occurred in the bush, we would have placed padded looped cables around it at intervals and winched. The underside could then be scooped out and filled with reinforcement, after which the cables could be simultaneously loosened.

Back in Florence late that afternoon, I returned to the hotel, opened the door, hiked the 14 flights, jammed the bread knife into my room door catch and decided on a hot water shave. I was to be ready for the flight the next morning to Rome. Stumbling into the darkened bathroom, I turned on the hot tap and wet the brush. The water was now freezing, so I completed the shave as I would have in the bush.

Next morning, after I had dried the arm which I had used to grope about in the cistern and rolled down the sleeve, I made the 14-flight descent for the last time. I ate my horseshoes and jam, returned the bread knife and key to the manager, and paid my bill. His face appeared to say 'it's really a shame to take the money.'

As we circled overhead in the plane, I was almost sure I caught a glimpse of my hotel. At least in Florence the statues of petrified people were well made.

Chapter 16

SPAGHETTI & GREECE

J UST as I thought, the flight to Rome was once again the usual
150 miles. In a short while we were back on the ground at the
airport. A taxi driver grabbed my bag from where the bus had
stranded me, so I showed him the name of the listed hotel, *Pensione
Patrizia*. We were off all in the same action and after a wild ride
lasting a few minutes, we stopped outside the hotel. The driver
dumped the bag in the gutter and asked for 800 lire. This seemed
a lot for so short a ride, so while he waited fuming, I took out my
cardboard slide rule to discover it was almost 10/- and showed
him the instrument. He insisted on his original fee. As a crowd
started gathering I gave him a 1,000 lire note. He put it in his dirty
white dust coat muttering, and went to drive away, but I slapped at
his arm and repeated '800' which made him really mad. I reckoned
he had already taken me for twice the tip, so I wouldn't let him go

until he fumbled in every pocket. He hopped from one foot to the other and finally jabbed a 100 lire coin at me. By now the crowd, sounding more like a tribe of aborigines during a corroboree, were all jabbering to each other. I didn't know whose side they were on, so I let him go and accepted the short change. It had become a matter of principle rather than value, but being from the bush I was rapidly losing ground anyway.

A hotel attendant went to pick up my bag, but with a similar scene in mind so soon, I brushed his hand away. I informed him that I wasn't paralysed, and went into the lobby. The man at the desk luckily had my name on his register, because I suspected I was already black-listed by the cabbies. At the same time I wondered just what I would do if any of these registers failed to include my name. I thought how thoroughly organised the airline booking people were. I hadn't arranged anything since the office in London had handed me the book of tickets.

I turned to see the bell boy already gripping my bag, so to save fighting him for it I went along with him to the iron-cage lift. This one worked all right, so up we went to the room. Feeling as hungry as I could without actually falling over, I asked him where I could get something to eat. Relieved to see he could understand me, I ate something in the dining room he directed me to, before setting out on my attack on Rome. Asking the clerk in the office where this hotel was located—in order that I could return home—he replied 'Via Nazionale.' I encouraged him by asking '...and then where?' All I seemed to be getting for weeks now were funny-looking stares from everybody.

Every place seemed to have its own special attraction to distinguish it. To me it was the Coliseum in Rome. Heading off down the street, a *Via* according to the map I had secured from the desk, I was detained by a man in a huge overcoat, despite the heat of the day. He whispered to me in an undertone of English, asking if I wanted to buy some cameos, after which he showed me a card full of them from his coat pocket. I didn't even know what they were. When I explained to him that I wouldn't be able to make much use of them, he went on to another item and another and another until I found he was a veritable mobile curio shop.

The pockets of his outsized overcoat bulged with his wares, with dozens of articles pinned to the inside. After I told him I didn't need any of these, I resumed walking again, but he lowered his whisper and informed me he had some very expensive pens he had 'got on the black' and wondered if I was interested. I told him I had many pens already, that I had got on the *white*. He quoted me a price, nevertheless, so I took out the slide rule, told him it was still no, and continued. He followed saying he would give me two for the same money, and opened his inner coat to reveal rows of them in plastic bags. I must have walked for a mile with him following until his price was wavering I could now have four pens for the same. Another half-mile and he asked me just what I would give to get rid of him, so I quoted a price which would barely compensate him for his worn shoe leather, but he immediately jumped at it and I became the owner of a 'hot' pen for a few shillings. The pen proved so hot that when I got it back to Australia, it melted into a toffee-like substance as we watched.

THE rain had so thoroughly washed the Coliseum during the few thousand years of its existence, that no trace of blood was left when I got there. I had read that the opening *day* of the arena was a blood bath which lasted for three months. Every time the activity slackened, they would throw another person to the lions, which were herded into cubicles under the floor. The floor was missing now and the lion warren was revealed to view. It was a shame to see the effects of the earthquake, which had shattered part of it, necessitating the shored-up modern brickwork. I was sure it would have taken nothing short of a huge tremor to have caused damage.

Inside St. Peter's Basilica in the Vatican City, I felt out of place for once, wearing my desert boots. However, they did make it easier to climb to the top of the famous dome for an impressive bird's eye view of Rome. A little later at the Forum, I was idly looking at the black cats which inhabited the ancient ruins, when two men ambled over to lean on a rail beside me. I knew they had come from Texas without even looking up, as one slowly drawled to his *Pardner*, 'Yes sirree; right thar by that coyote bait is sure where Julius Caesar got his'n.' Looking up, I saw that the other had pushed his big hat to the back of his head before replying 'Shucks! He couldn't have been too quick on the draw!' After which the pair bow-legged away, chuckling over the joke.

That night, returning home dog tired after a full day's hiking, I remembered that my friend in the special security group who handled the secrecy involved for the atomic blast in Australia six years before, had mentioned that he would be posted to Rome. Studying the phone book, I searched for the name Leo Carter. Sure enough, it was listed, so I dialled the number. I could hardly stand up at the phone, hanging as it was on a wall, hungry and tired as I felt. Soon a voice answered with one clipped word 'Carter.' He always had to be tight-lipped due to his profession, so I answered with my name, wondering if he would believe me as I hadn't seen him since the bomb trials in South Australia. As I anticipated, I heard a sort of choking sound followed by an incredulous query, as to what I was doing in Rome. I told him I was talking to him on a telephone, which seemed to me an accurate enough statement. In twenty minutes he had driven his Mercedes *via Nationale* to the hotel I had described. Not being able to pronounce it, I explained it was opposite a certain sort of neon sign.

After the welcome, he continued to drive me around the city until the early hours of the morning, pointing out the things I never would have been able to see on foot. I was due to leave the following day. There were statues of muscular 'Mr Italy' fighting with rocky serpents and a waterhole where the film *Three coins in the Fountain* had been made. Another place looked very like a Red Indian's camp, with rows of stone totem poles, each with somebody's head on top. At first, in the gloom, it looked like a parade of people dressed in rolls of lino. Then came a cage with a wolf in it, pacing back and forth continuously, like a professor giving a lecture. Leo explained that wolves were something very special to Rome.

One stop we made was near a great block of rock, with five white sausage-shaped rocks on top of it, looking rather like loaves of bread on a tray. On examining it further I noticed they were all joined to one big rock, which was shaped very much like an ankle. Leo explain to me that the 'loaves of bread' were toes and this was one foot of the statue of a man.

A block of apartments next to a famous flight of stairs had doors leading out on to the footpath. One of these was especially pointed out to be where Keats had lived. A small schoolboy in Sydney, who had answered a poetry question in an examination, could never have visited Rome. The question had instructed the candidates to 'write all you know about Keats' and the small boy had replied 'I don't know anything; I don't even know what they are.' I was then shown a small balcony overlooking the square on which Mussolini used to stand to chat to the people early in the war.

Crossing and re-crossing the large creek running through the city by car was certainly easier than it had been on foot. Finally, Leo drove me back to the hotel, after explaining the creek was really the Tiber River. It had been a wonderful addition to the visit and I was very grateful for Leo's kindness, although he told me I should have contacted him the moment I arrived. As he drove off I noticed another burst water main spraying water out of the middle of the street, but being so very hungry I didn't have the strength to further investigate it. Instead, I asked the clerk about it, and he glared at me in a horrified way. He informed me that it was one of the most well-known fountains in Rome. Too weak to get up for breakfast, I was forced to miss it and urged myself to fill in the time before the airport bus departure, by walking over to the airline office, under the neon sign opposite the hotel. On the way past the desk I paid the bill of 6,700 lire in lire notes, each of which was large enough in area to wrap a serve of fish and chips. After systematically extracting tips from me during my stay, the manager at the desk asked me for some extra lire for himself. Pointing out the large word *servizio* already on the bill, I picked up the bag and headed off out the door with more agility than I felt.

The time came to drag myself into the airport, feeling as if I had eaten nothing for days, which in fact was the case. I never seemed to know where to go for a meal in these big cities. Eventually, after seeing the broken aqueducts on the way, and climbing into the plane, we were circling over the city where, according to another schoolboy's answer to a question, 'Mark Anthony had given Cleopatra a jewel case with her entrails engraved on the lid.'

'Yes-siree…right there is where Julius got him.'

AS we were soon over the sea, my first impression was that we were flying in the wrong direction, meaning the plane was west of Rome. From a plot on the map I knew we had to travel south of east if we were to reach Athens. I told a couple from Chicago seated opposite me and they agreed after I showed them my map, leaving us to imagine something sinister was going on 'up front'. Soon, however, the aircraft banked and flew in the opposite direction, back towards the land. The couple from Chicago agreed we must have made a circle to gain height, before making the trip. No one else in the plane seemed aware of all this drama and if they had noticed it at all, they would have known it was standard procedure.

Being a B.E.A. flight, I was quite relieved to see that the hostess was English. When she brought a snack of sandwiches to the passengers, I had mine finished before my friends opposite had the wrapping off theirs. When they saw that, they both handed me their rations—which I devoured—as well as drinking their cups of tea. The man from the windy city called out to the passengers on the other side of the aisle to inform them that 'this guy is starving,' which resulted in a further issue of sandwiches and tea. The hostess noticed this as well, and brought along a bundle of six more packets which I ate without stopping for breath. From the wrappings they told me I'd eaten 15 packets of sandwiches and had drunk nine cups of tea. With tears in her eyes, an old lady went over and added hers. I explained that since the chocolate coins at Zurich Airport, I had only eaten several bread horseshoes and some mugs of water.

Six and a half hundred miles later, in the night, we landed in Athens. Riding in the taxi to the *Hôtel D'Athènes* with the Chicago couple, I was already in possession of a bucketful of drachmas. They looked like being handy, as I noticed the array of big new sparkling cars everywhere, making me think I would need it all. I went up to my room at the hotel. Strengthened by my supper on the plane, I came down again, as late as it was, and walked around for a first look at Athens.

Neon signs brightly lit the squares and main streets. They were all spelling out words using the Greek alphabet. I could recognise several of the symbols, having used them for many years in the prefixes for star names in their constellations, while plotting my way through the deserts of outback Australia, using astronomical observations.

Ambling past one dimly-lit doorway, a uniformed man approached and enquired if I'd care to go down the stairs for a quiet cup of coffee. He told me it was a peaceful place, where visitors could relax and listen to music. It was still beyond me how everyone knew I was a visitor, but I thought it was very good of him to consider me in the first place. Halfway down the stairs I noticed a girl sitting at a table at the bottom, making me glad on her behalf that the weather was warm. Dressed like that she could have otherwise easily caught a chill. Another step and I could see several others, when suddenly the first one glanced sideways up at me, winked and beckoned me down into the room. At this, I turned and leapt up the stairs four at a time, to emerge back on to the footpath alongside the uniformed doorman. In answer to his query, I explained I had gone halfway before coming back. He stared at me with his jaw hanging open and exclaimed in genuine disbelief '...and you came out again?' I explained I had just had nine mugs of tea and suddenly didn't really feel thirsty. As I wandered off, I could understand his amazement, as not many people he would have met had just had nine cups of tea, but it was useless to try to explain it all to him. I then walked for hours trying to find my hotel, not being able to ask anyone. At last I recognised a neon sign with its capital Σ, so went straight to my hotel. In my room—while positioning my camera on the window ledge for a time exposure photograph of the blaze of signs—I noticed directly across the street, the doorman standing by the open door, with a flight of steps behind it. It was then I realised I could have been home in three minutes, instead of hiking for hours.

I headed for the Acropolis to see the Parthenon, which seemed to be near enough to where our civilisation had its beginnings. On the way up the hill a man pounced upon me and offered to guide me around the ruins, and explain them all for a handful of drachmas. Knowing he'd be able to tell me more about it than I could discover in the time, I went along with him and as it turned out, he was very helpful. With all that wonderful stonework underneath, I wondered what they had used as roofing. There was a great deal more involved in this structure than I thought, as I gathered from the old Greek, who explained that the foundations were curved in such a way as to eliminate the distortion of perspective. It was altogether worth the trip and the handful of drachmas.

If a visitor could feel the atmosphere of the ruins, it added greatly to know how the ancients chipped away at the stone, what they ate and how they slept at night. I wondered if they camped on the hill itself, or whether they had a camp remote from the job. If so, how far away, and how did they travel to and from work? There were other things of interest to consider, like what tools they used and what sort of instruments to set out their work so precisely.

Many people must have worked a lifetime endeavouring to answer these questions. I found myself walking away feeling very much at a loss. That afternoon at Sounion I realised just how much thought must have gone into the buildings, when I was told that the columns contained one more concave flute than the ones at the Parthenon. This made the angles of the junctions slightly more blunt, so helping the stone to withstand the depredations of the sea, sand and winds from the nearby coast.

Before light next morning, we left for another bus trip to an island south of the mainland. It had the name of Peloponnese printed across it on the map. It wasn't an island until a channel was cut through the narrow strip of land once joining it to the mainland. Boats could now pass through and a bridge took the traffic. The strip of land looked narrow on the map, but on viewing the canal it must have been a sizeable engineering project. It would have been easy enough for the ancients.

Seeing the spots where St. Paul once preached to the people at Nauplia, and where they were known to have later dragged him, gave a newcomer to the area quite a strange sort of feeling. For those who lived there it was probably just part of their everyday environment. At a well-known stone opening known as the *Gateway of the Lionesses* there were still parallel ruts in the road, which were the tracks left by the chariots. It was so well-known that I had never heard of it, but the carvings of lionesses were still as good as ever on the stone lintel over the gate.

One set of seats, made in a perfect part-circle, shaped around a sunken stage, was to be seen at a place called Epidaurus. Anyone whispering on the stage below could be heard all over this acoustic theatre. I didn't discover what sort of plays were put on, or for what duration, but after sitting on one of the stone seats—and thinking how very cold and hard they were—I wondered if the audience brought along their own pillows or suffered in silence.

Someone had worked out that there should be some tombs under the rocky overburden in one spot. After much study, he had dug down and found them, proving he had been right, and also showing how much information could be gleaned from ancient records.

On the way back to Athens after dark, the bus collected a flat tyre. This caused the Greek driver to become most upset. His yelling told everyone just how disappointed he was. Here, however, was something I could understand, after half a lifetime in the bush, so I went with him to help to change it. He was really quite a genial fellow, I decided during the operation, after working on him as well as the tyre.

Arriving in Athens, I kept thinking there was something I had to do that night. On glancing at my book of tickets, I suddenly remembered. It was to fly to Africa. The plane was due to leave at midnight, so collecting my bag at the hotel, I paid the desk clerk 205 drachmas, then humped the bag on my shoulder to the airline office in the city. Checking it in, I discovered the time I was to be ready and waiting: midnight. With a little time left, I made a further expedition on foot around the town.

While passing a respectable-looking establishment opposite a small paddock in the centre of the main part of the city, I noticed another strong-looking uniformed doorman standing on the footpath. He was near the top of a flight of stairs. He came over and blocked my path as I approached. He cheerfully asked me if I'd care to relax over a cup of coffee, and all but pushed me to the head of the stairs. Blocking my exit, he began lumbering down after me. To prevent being crushed, I edged down in front of him. Turning around, I couldn't help but notice a rather easy-to-look-at young lady at a mirror placed at a right angle turn in the staircase. Her costume, made as it was from mosquito net, reminded me of the style worn by fairies. As we descended, she just happened to be preening herself in front of the glass. She turned and the smile she gave me made me explain suddenly to the uniformed man that I just remembered I had to be off to another place. I must have convinced him, as he momentarily turned sideways. In that instant I squeezed past him and raced up the stairs, as he bellowed after me 'where?' As I reached the top, and skidded around into the street, gripping the hand rail to keep my balance, I twisted around and called back my one word answer: 'Africa!'

Chapter 17

THE GAME NEEDS PROTECTING

I THOUGHT I was back home when I opened my eyes and viewed the scene below. The increasing drone of the engines had put me into a deep sleep upon leaving Athens. After flying all night, sleeping in the fork of the seats, I felt like a koala bear.

Drowsily settling back into the fork again, the fact suddenly struck me that I wasn't due home for another three weeks, so jumping up and pulling back the curtains once more, I saw it again. Sandhills stretching out to the horizon, made up of a shimmering heat haze in every direction, with nothing else to be seen. The plane corrected itself after a slight bank, giving me a fleeting glimpse of a creek winding through the dunes, with small patches of greenery on either side. This settled the fact that it wasn't Central Australia: no such water supply existed there, but even so the sand dunes at home had more growth on them than here.

The sound of the intercom being switched on from the cockpit woke me. The pilot spoke, informing us we were over the Sahara Desert, flying along the White Nile. A look at the map supplied by South African Airways, revealed that I must have slept over Egypt. We were now in Sudan. The aeroplane began to descend nearer to the sand, which made me realise how long it had been since I had seen this familiar open country.

Landing on the strip at Khartoum, where the Blue Nile joins the White, the heat became evident as soon as the doors were opened. It was just like climbing out of a survey reconnaissance plane after landing on one of my own homemade airfields in the bush. It was good to have the wall of dry heat greet me at the doorway. Everyone here was wearing double sheets, leaving only their ankles and eyes bare. The overall effect looked to me as if a number of tents—minus the pegs—were moving about. At the same time I thought it to be a most effective sort of clothing for the desert, but if I had worn the same in Australia the aborigines would have run for miles at the sight of me.

I forced myself to wait until the aircraft was refuelled instead of automatically wandering straight off into the desert. By this time the machine had heated to the usual oven-like temperature, as we had so often experienced. With a sigh and an envious backward look at the 'ghosts' we were soon airborne, with the coolers on the plane helping the passengers forget such a place existed.

Grazing the western tip of the Ethiopian border, we were now in Kenya. We crossed the equator, where groups of circular, pointed grass huts made up the villages. Landing at the Nairobi aerodrome in the early afternoon, I produced my visitor's pass, allowing me to enter. It would also permit me to go to Zanzibar, as long as I didn't seek employment. It was a handy thing to have, because you never knew when you might suddenly get an urge to go to Zanzibar. It also worked for Tanganyika.

I phoned the couple I had met in Venice, Graham and June Ward, who kindly came around to where I was staying at the New Stanley Hotel. They drove me to their home, where I was given a lot of first-hand information about the place.

The driving licence which I had used legally in the UK, Switzerland and the Nullarbor Plain, didn't, for some unknown reason, operate here. I hiked up to the High Commissioner's place and purchased a temporary one for 30/-. While booking and paying for a flight to Serengeti in Tanganyika, scheduled in a few day's time, I called into the survey office in Nairobi. The surveyors, on learning of my own work in Australia, immediately sent for a driver with a Landrover, to show me over the game reserve close by. At every stop a group of loud-mouthed baboons leapt on to the vehicle bonnet and roof, and played at sliding down the windscreen. One of them sat on the bonnet and stared at me, so I just stared right back. I was hoping he didn't know me from somewhere. A zebra crossing the road made us stop as is usual in cities, then he joined his mob not far away from a giraffe munching away at the top foliage of a tree. There was another hungry-looking animal in the middle of eating a lioness at another stop. The driver thought it was a cheetah, whereas to me it looked like an oversized dingo, but whatever it was, I would have felt more at home wearing my revolver. An ostrich, with muscular bare pink thighs, obviously couldn't stand the sight of us and jammed his head into the ground. Later we saw a rat-like pig—or a pig-like rat—burrowing like fury into a bank at our approach.

Back in Nairobi, I was invited to have a Chinese tea with the Chief Surveyor, Harry Williams and his family. I asked them what the animal was which had been casually devouring the lioness. The response included any one of quite a variety of animals whose diets often included lionesses for their main meals. I drew a picture of the predator from memory on a paper serviette. This was slowly handed around, from table to table, throughout the whole dining room. Everybody studiously gave their opinions and it settled the topic of conversation for the entire evening. I asked one learned-looking man if it could quite possibly be a bunyip, but after long consideration, he decided it wasn't one of these. After that, I must confess I didn't have the heart to advise him of the old Australian legend. The drawing was eventually pinned on the wall for anyone who would care to add his opinion.

I CALLED for the car I had hired early next morning, and drove north a hundred miles to Nyeri to visit the *Tree Tops Hotel*— which I had heard about. It had branches growing out through the walls, and from the rooms I could see night owls and big game drinking at a waterhole.

On the way I resumed my usual role of bus driver, picking up hitchhikers. The difference this time was that they were African schoolchildren. On one section of mud road, a team was working with bulldozers, and as I slid down the grade, I idly wondered how I was going to get back up again on the return trip. Eventually, driving to a place called the *Outspan Hotel,* which had been mentioned by Graham and June, I discovered that Charlie Chaplin had already been there before me. It was, however, mainly remembered as a home of Lord Baden-Powell, the founder of the world-wide scout movement. He had based much of the organisation upon the habits of the animals he had studied right here where he had spent so many years.

I was just in time to leave the Austin I had hired, and transfer to a safari truck for the trip further out to *Treetops* to spend the night. There was still ample time to pay the 155/- before we headed off with my companions: a most jolly American couple. I was able to make them feel less homesick on the twelve-mile trip, with the story of the con man in LA. The truck couldn't get beyond a certain point, so we all got out and mooched up through the jungle the rest of the way, like a line of cows at milking time.

The building was constructed on the top of some trees near a billabong, with several logs upright for support like Queensland houses. We trooped up to it using a set of steps. Apparently there had been another such building on the other side of the waterhole, but the mau-mau had decided to burn it down. The present structure was the second attempt. Where the other building used to be, a sign had been attached to the trunk of the mgumu tree, which had been left after the fire. It informed visitors that it was in that original *Treetops* that Her Royal Highness, Princess Elizabeth and the Duke of Edinburgh had spent the night of the 5th February, 1952. While there, the Princess had succeeded to the throne of England, on the death of her father, King George VI.

As this area was on the equator, the animals camped during the day and ambled out to drink during the cooler evenings. A permanent 'full moon' had been made, to hang from the verandah, in the form of a lamp and reflector behind a yellowish frosted glass. This was to show the animals to visitors in a better light. I wondered what the animals thought each month when a real full moon was also in the sky. One way to prevent the animals suspecting their waterhole had been 'spiked' would have been to switch off the artificial moon.

After dark, the baboons came for their small sip before some great elephant drained it through his trunk. With absolute quietness prevailing in the trees where we sat, a rhinoceros lumbered up, licked at the salt specially sprinkled about and plodded on into the water to quench his sudden thirst. As we watched him there, quietly minding his own business, a second one shuffled into the 'moonlight.' For no reason at all, he dragged his bulk over to the first rhino. He did his level best to ram the spike on his nose into his opponent's stomach. It seemed a thoroughly unkind thing to do. The first rhino must have had a nice nature, proved by the fact that he did not even glance up. Finally, after six more savage attempts to administer the injection, the nasty-natured rhino licked up some salt and commenced his drink. The pain we felt watching all this must have finally taken effect on the slow brain of the first rhino, who lifted his head out of the water just long enough to return the injection.

A buffalo filled the limelight with its size. It was followed by a hog, and the night was divided up into watching their antics and huddling up in a blanket as the cold closed in. Early next morning the 'moon' was switched off. Walking around the tree trunk growing out through the middle of the lounge room floor, we went back to the *Outspan* for breakfast, where I reclaimed the Austin for the drive back to Nairobi.

There must have been more rain during the night, as the slippery road held no traction for the wheels in the mud. When I came to the freshly bulldozed section, several cars were stationary, quite unable to pass the obstruction. One of the heaps alongside the road consisted mainly of rock, so I drove onto it with one set of tyres partially deflated. Everyone followed the wheel tracks. I had already decided to start the bulldozer and planned to drag everyone over with it—if the attempt had proven unsuccessful. Stopping later for several more schoolchildren, I became very badly bogged. While they sat comfortably in the car, I tugged away the soft mud with my hands, to replace it with stones.

I handed a mud-caked car back to the owners in Nairobi and decided that the firm must have been quite used to this: they didn't even make a comment about it.

After hammering off the blocks of dried mud from my arms and feet with the end of a mop handle—used like a crowbar—and wiping the desert boots on the other end of the mop, I went to have dinner at the luxurious dining room in *New Stanley*. Having had nothing to eat since breakfast at the *Outspan*, I was early. Some violinists were playing, even before people began to arrive. It sounded complicated music to me, I thought as I attacked the meal in front of me. One of the musicians stopped playing and came over to my table. He said that I looked lonely and asked for a request which they would be very happy to play for me. I was at a complete loss to even suggest anything as complicated as the music they seemed to be playing. As I was wondering how to get out of the situation, some people arrived, so I told him I'd let them ask first. With my meal over, I slipped out as quickly as I could, unobserved by the musicians in case I was asked again.

THE Dakota was ready and waiting at the airport the next day for the take off to Serengeti in Tanganyika. It wasn't long before we were flying past the snow-capped 19,340-foot Mt. Kilimanjaro, near Kenya's southern border. Pointed circular huts were still the fashion near the landing strip, and on collecting some food from one of them, we transferred to a larger safari wagon with boarded sides. We were soon away on a hundred-mile trip to see some of the animals in Tanganyika. At last I was the only one wearing the most appropriate clothes, with my shorts, belt and hunting knife. I felt I would have increased in size from a penknife to a much larger affair had I been living there.

A lioness lounged under the shade of a tree and, as we were accidentally between her and some cubs, it didn't seem to be a good idea to climb down for a photograph. Allegedly, one person did once, and the lioness ate the photographer, spitting out the camera like a pip as she chewed. Some lions—mops of hair around their necks—were mooching across the prairie. I concluded that I would need to adjust my usual bush camping style, if I had to work in this area. Instead of sleeping on the ground in a swag roll I would camp in an army tank.

I was sitting next to an old bearded man who had just left the Congo. Although he hadn't wanted to leave, he was forced to for health reasons. He told me some of the animals there were very unhealthy. He kept up a low undertone of explanation all the time. I heard about a quarter of it, the rest lost in the rattling of the truck.

Buffaloes and zebra were always to be seen. In one waterhole a hippopotamus was kind enough to show us an inch of his back. It looked more like a submerged lump of granite. We had a dinner camp beside a creek on the way. It had rapids in it, and as usual in such circumstances one of the tourists managed to fall in, slipping on a rock while attempting to cross over. My old friend from the Congo laughed so hard that his large helmet fell off and was carried downstream at great speed.

Dinner seemed to come to a rather untimely conclusion when a friendly boa constrictor eased through the sword grass and on to the bank. I turned around to mention it to someone sitting next to me, when I suddenly found I was completely on my own. I quickly joined the others in the wagon and we moved away at a leisurely forty miles per hour.

IT was altogether a good trip and after seeing several lions and a cheetah—or bunyip—we drove back to the airfield. One inhabitant of the pointed huts asked me how I liked the place. I was quite truthful in telling him I'd certainly like to do some survey work out here. His asked what game we had seen during the trip. I mentioned the lioness and snake, and added that I had been waiting all day to see some kangaroos and was very sad to have missed them. She turned serious and explained carefully that if I wanted to see those, well then I'd have to go to Australia. I thanked her very much, and told her how grateful I was for the information. I then took out a paper and pencil and wrote as she watched: 'Australia for cangaroos.' She then hastened to point out to me that it was spelt with a 'k.' After crossing out my effort and correcting it, I told her how very kind she had been. For once my home country had not been spotted by just looking at me. I began to feel concerned that I had been away too long.

Circling over the reserve near Nairobi we saw a row of cars forming a perfect circle, with the bonnets towards the centre. In the small ring thus formed a zebra lay dead, with two lions tearing it to pieces. They seemed quite oblivious to the infringement on their privacy during their afternoon tea break. We flew so low that I noticed all the car windows were tightly shut.

After telling Graham and June about my trip, I went off to see Nairobi itself. I happened upon an art exhibition where an English lady was endeavouring to sell her paintings. She walked around with me, and on the way asked if I did any drawing myself.

I replied that I did. She immediately asked if I held any art exhibitions. Thinking of the sketches I did for survival in France and how they had been later pinned up in the kitchen of the Hotel d'Iéna, I casually told her I was at present showing in Paris, as well as other parts of the continent. She asked in an awed whisper what type of subjects I had chosen. I informed her they were mostly studies in still life.

CALLING in to the Survey Office of the Lands Department, I walked past a man who stopped me and threw down his survey bag. I noticed that his jaw had dropped open when he first caught sight of me. When he managed to shut it again he slapped me on the back and wrung my hand yelling out 'If it isn't Lennie Beadell.' I didn't know him at all, but it appeared that he once lived in New South Wales. I used to take his small son out for trips in my car, when near his area. He still couldn't believe his eyes. We had quite a good chat about those days, which were really only a few years ago. He insisted I come home with him for tea. It was only there that I discovered his name was Alec Taylor. It was wonderful to be amongst Australians once again.

Finally, arranging to see him for supper I returned to the New Stanley. As I was due to leave Nairobi that night, I booked the

Austin once more for a final look at the animals in the game reserve during my last afternoon.

On the way to collect the car, I saw a man being kicked out of a bus. As he was flying through the air I realised I hadn't often seen *that* happen before. I mentally retraced his trajectory to the boot which did the kicking. The boot was withdrawn as the bus drove away. Apparently a difference of opinion had cropped up between the driver, conductor and passenger, as they went past me. Suddenly the bus stopped in the middle of the street, the door flew open and, while one held the passenger in place, the other kicked him out into the gutter. This unfortunate human football picked himself up and, judging by the way he shook his fist and screamed after the departing vehicle, I gathered that the whole incident had disturbed him.

Later on at the reserve the African to whom I had given a lift and I saw two lions in the grass finishing their afternoon tea. My companion told me the meal was composed of a couple of gnus. Here was a case where one of them could have easily repeated the phrase often heard on the radio, 'This is the end of the gnus.'

Alec Taylor drove me to the aerodrome later in the evening. With only minutes to spare, I phoned the couple I had met in Venice to thank them for their kindness and to say goodbye.

There followed a six-hour flight back over the equator to Aden. We landed just long enough for the aircraft to refuel and for somebody to steal the fountain pen from my coat on my seat. They didn't worry about the knife, which I used for scalping dingoes, which was in the same pocket.

It was then onwards over the Arabian Sea for another six-hour flight. At midday we circled over Bombay. I had just two weeks of this expedition left to go.

Chapter 18

BACK TO THE BUSH

THIS was the very city which gave rise to the saying: 'the climate of Bombay is such that its inhabitants have to live elsewhere.' Although this came from the pencil of a small child, who had never been here, I could see what he meant. We made the bus trip from the airport through the humidity and heat to the Taj Mahal Hotel.

The hotel looked all right to me, being one of the most impressive buildings I had yet seen. Apparently its architect didn't think so, being reputed to have committed suicide by jumping off the second floor during its construction. He lived somewhere else and the construction had commenced from his plans. It rose to the second floor before he made a visit to inspect it. I was told that the chap who laid out the foundations had somehow reversed the drawings, thus putting the back doors facing the waterfront.

The elaborate design, meant to be in full view, was hidden at the rear. All the intricate work, which was to be seen by all from the harbour, was lost to view in a back alley. This proved too much for him and he flung himself from the top of the building to his death. I could understand how sad he must have felt, but there was no need for him to throw himself into his work.

In the dining room where I gathered strength for the attack, I noticed some wonderfully coloured statues arranged on the tables. I lost count of the number of fans, big and small, around the room. They were all going full blast and the effect was that of a haven from the sticky humidity. During the meal something seemed to be gradually happening to the statues. By the time I'd finished they had shrunk to half size. Walking past the main table where they were displayed, I discovered they were made of ice, and were now standing on their knees in a bath of coloured water. It reminded me that I had done the very same thing myself in Paris the month before.

BACK into the heat again, I started walking, to use what was left of the afternoon and evening. Ambling out of the back door—which was really the front door—around to the front where the back door was, I was set upon by several small children begging. Although they looked pitifully thin and pleaded with such urgency, I forced myself to walk on. I had been strongly advised not to give to beggars by the hotel desk clerk. They learned from birth how to beg so convincingly. The offer of just one small coin would bring crowds of them descending upon an unsuspecting visitor, resulting in all-out fights for possession. It had been almost an *order* not to give, and it was a hard job to adhere to it, although anyone could see sense in the reasons given.

As dusk drew on, I found I was stepping over an ever-increasing number of bodies sleeping at all angles across the footpaths and in gutters, half covered by bags or torn dirty rags for blankets. One very old woman was plodding along, clutching a piece of blanket the size of a bath towel. As I watched, she lay down on the concrete where she stopped, pulled the tattered rag over her shoulders and settled down for the night. I was told that some of these people never wake up, and are collected the following day.

I started hiking in earnest first thing the next morning, wondering how many miles I had walked altogether on this trip. I started off on Mahatma Gandhi Road. Next I dragged myself up the hill past the hanging gardens to a paddock overlooking the Towers of Silence. When I first heard about these hanging gardens, I wondered how all the soil stayed in place, but it appeared that only the *herbage* was hanging.

The paddock on top was full of animals, but I was relieved—having just come from Tanganyika—to see they were all made of clipped hedges. A vertical sundial was attached to a stone. Having recently finished the calculations for a horizontal sundial to decorate an Australian sheep station homestead, I studied it for so long that I was afraid of being arrested for loitering. A square tower on the northern end of the paddock seemed to be constantly under attack from vultures soaring overhead, and it wasn't until during the afternoon that I saw why.

On top of the same hill I found a boot on the grass, which wasn't unusual in itself, apart from the fact that this one had a balcony over the laces, and a gabled roof complete with chimney on top of the opening for the ankle bones, twenty feet up from the ground. Had it been in Rome, this Mother Hubbard's boot would have just about fitted the man with the 'loaves of bread' toes, who must have taken at least a size 88.

I saw an old bus full of Indians lumbering in the direction I wanted to go home. Not feeling brisk enough to make it on foot, I climbed in and sat on the floor, with all the turban-topped passengers. No air was coming in to this oven-like vehicle, chock-full with shimmering fumes from bodies, sweat and dirt, but I noticed they at least put up with me.

Standing on the back steps—at the front of the hotel, deciding which way to go, a white-uniformed attendant approached and asked if I'd like to hire a taxi for the afternoon, with him as guide and interpreter. I hesitated, thinking this would cost more than I had change for, when he explained the full cost would be 20 rupees. The card given by the hotel explaining the currency showed me this was only 30/- so I accepted immediately.

He showed me places I could never have found on my own. I saw where the religious offered gifts of food, which they placed on a mat at the entrance to a most extravagant temple. Hundreds of women were washing clothes in the open, each using the concrete trough allotted to them. The whole area was called the Dohobi Ghard. The guide explained how they collected and delivered the clothes in a hand cart. They ran about Bombay like cost-plus contractors, getting as much work as there was daylight for.

In another area of the poor markets, rows of people sat all over the roadway with vegetables spread about on dirty rags, selling their meagre stocks to customers. Across the road were dozens of cubicles constructed of bagging, where people were having haircuts. There were no clippers or scissors involved, only razors, making the clients look as if they had just survived a hair attack.

Driving through this milling mass of humanity would have been impossible without a loud horn, and our driver rarely had his hand off the button. He then took me to one of the most amazing places where huts were built behind a high rock wall, and through an iron gate where people called *Untouchables* lived. They weren't allowed to go out during their lifetime, their goods being brought to them. Their sole purpose on earth was to handle the dead bodies of people, placing them on the sunken roof of the tower which I had seen from the paddock on the hill. The vultures would swoop in and eat the remains in a few minutes, then wait for the next, as their religion taught the Hindus that nothing should ever be wasted. Untouchables were not allowed to have any contact with outsiders, and their children were born to inherit the task for their own life's duration. The vultures were always circling and waiting, to be seen by everyone, and I looked at these people lying about, also waiting. Some of the rich people would be buried in most expensive-looking tombs. The population certainly exhibited extremes of wealth and poverty.

Complete families lived in sheds made entirely of bags along the railway line, while others lived under rag awnings tied to fences or walls and held down in the gutter with stones. Walking along these streets pedestrians were forced to use the roadway. One such family I photographed waited until I climbed back in the car, at which time the guide allowed me to press some coins into the filthy little outstretched hands of one of the children. As soon as I did so the driver was off like a rocket, while we were still able.

After paying the man his twenty rupees that night—some of which he gave to the taxi driver—I went for a walk down a particularly dark lane which I had noticed earlier. Here were tiny humpies made of tin and bag, some of which had a dim light from a fat lamp outside, revealing the heaps of people jammed into them. It was here they lived all their lives. I penetrated the gloom cast by the fat lamps for a hundred yards, before deciding to evacuate while I could, although I had left everything from my pockets back at the hotel.

Struggling, bone-weary, past the huge rock arch of the *Gateway of India* the next morning, I almost fell into a boat tied nearby, for a visit to a basalt island. It was here the old *Elephants Caves* had been carved into bedrock in the eighth century, twelve hundred years ago. The man-made caves were lined with deep carvings of faces and snakes, which have survived as good as new in the gloom. I wondered what they had used for tools and illumination to carry out the work to such perfection.

Back again at the desk of the Taj Mahal Hotel, after paying my bill of 60 rupees and 50 naye paise, I asked the clerk if I could obtain a set of their coins. Having some gleaming new ones already, I asked if he could let me have others in such good condition. He sorted out everything but a 10 naye paise coin, which looked dull and old. He excused himself and rushed off, returning with a rag and tin of metal polish, which he used to make the shoddy coin sparkle. I decided that they were indeed a very polite and helpful people.

THE Comet 4 jet started on the thousand-mile trip to Colombo that afternoon, for a view of where all the tea we drink in the bush comes from. In a couple of hours we were on the ground in Ceylon. At the Galle Face Hotel, where the airline said I was to camp that night, a Californian doctor and his wife, who had just rushed in from the pyramids, were trying to hire a car with driver, to make a several-hundred mile excursion to some distant spots in Ceylon. He was on a lightning holiday trip apparently. As I was at the desk for much the same reason, we got together, each paying a third. Constantly enquiring if this arrangement would suit me, I assured him it was the very best for all concerned. With that, out came the recent photograph taken of them both on camels, with the pyramids in the background. His wife supplied information about his work in California, constantly helped, as he was, by a bevy of young nurses. She added with a sigh that he expected the same treatment away from his surgery. She then went on to ask about me. I told her about my work in the Australian bush, where I didn't see anyone at all and didn't think I could expect the same away from it.

WE headed off on the Kandy road at dawn, after paying the hotel manager 40 rupees for the night. We charged out and into the car waiting outside, driven by a Sinhalese known as Wilson.

The doctor had shot a complete roll of film before we had even cleared Colombo. I was in possession of a single picture of an ox dragging a covered wagon along the street. Judging by the speed it was going, I figured we would be in Kandy, 60 miles away in Central Ceylon, before the rig made it to the end of the block. His wife said she hoped I didn't mind stopping all the time for pictures. Clough, her husband, was very keen on taking home a record of their trips, having already taken many thousands of slides on this outing. She added that they never had time to look at any of them. I was only too pleased at his enthusiasm; he would let me click off my four or five slides too.

Wilson was a great help, explaining everything as we drove—as if a demon were after us—and stopped cheerfully for each photo requested. He pointed out the ginger growing with the pepper, cocoa and coffee plants. Each of these merited five more pictures for Clough. At one bridge they sold sky rockets, three of which we were instructed by Wilson to buy. I wondered what part they played in the proceedings. Stopping in the middle of the bridge, we were told to point our cameras at the foliage of an enormous tree, while the rockets were placed in holes drilled for them, and lit. At the first launch a flurry of flying foxes emerged. The second lift-off caused the same effect, and the third blast-off liberated the whole tree's population in quite a spectacular fashion. The doctor's trigger finger blurred on his camera button. From the hills at Kandy the famous *Temple of the Tooth* was pointed out, where Buddhists from all countries make special pilgrimages to view the tooth of Buddha. Wilson mentioned that Kandy was also recognised to be one of the most ideally-sited towns in the world, a fact we could readily understand.

Climbing to a height of 7,000 feet, where a place called Nuwara Eliya was perched, we went to the Grand Hotel for a night's camp.

In the dining room, where the male waiters all wore great combs in their hair, we ordered the food, and when it was brought the doctor called for the head man—also hiding under a comb. He asked if the milk in the jug had been pasteurised, if the spoons had been sterilised and whether the beef had been immunised. Being assured that everything was therapeutic, we began the meal. Later I asked for some oranges. When they came, I enquired if they had been steamed clean in an autoclave, which made Clough and his wife laugh till their glasses fell off. She said 'You must think we are the fussiest people' and I told her I didn't at all, only I thought we were being a bit careful when the doctor asked if the ice cubes for his drink had been boiled. He had just written out an accurate prescription for a drink on a paper serviette which he handed to the comb-carrier to have dispensed.

They called me into their room later to show me some of their souvenirs collected from Egypt. Clough took off a ring he was wearing and held it as though it might explode. A discussion followed and they finally agreed, after which he threw the ring into the air and she caught it as it fell. I wondered what was going on, until she handed it to me in half a dozen separate linked pieces. I was told if I could put it together, then I could keep it as a memento of our trip. At three o'clock the next morning, I was still working on it and fell asleep with the bits in my hand. At dawn they burst into my room to see me asleep, clutching the pieces, but they still gave it to me. It wasn't until I got back to the bush that I finally managed to re-assemble the ring, which they didn't know how to do themselves. This explained the discussion beforehand, which caused them to make their big decision.

It was still full moon when we were there. I could have legally sat up in a tree all night shooting bears and leopards, but that ring had decided on my night's activities. I wasn't altogether sure what I would have done with a leopard anyway.

First thing in the morning Wilson was outside waiting with the car in the mountain mist. We were off again like a prowl-car in LA, within minutes of finishing our sterilised breakfast of vaccinated chook and inoculated sausages.

A tea factory was on the way, amongst hills of plantations. In one room, trays of leaves were being dried on wire mesh. Another contained conical piles of tea leaves, heaped up on the wooden floor, with a man shovelling it on to a fine mesh. Behind this a large extractor fan sucked out the dust, allowing the cleaned leaves to fall on to the floor. Girls sat around each mound of tea and hand-separated the larger stalks. There was one man walking about like a foreman, who looked as if he had been also hand-picked for the job. He didn't need to bend to inspect the work. Being fully grown—and only three feet high—he potted about, disappearing at intervals behind the tea leaves, only to emerge several heaps further on. The girls could not see him anyway, as they were draped in white, covering all but their faces, feet and hands. At first glance it looked like a meeting of the Ku Klux Klan. In a separate building staff were employed tasting the various blends, drinking cups of tea all day—a job which could have been done by any government civil servant.

After seeing the baskets of leaves carried by the girls, we screamed to a stop to see some elephants taking a bath. Nine photos later, Wilson had us at a shed to view some dancing. Clough raced in to inspect a hospital at a stop overlooking oxen in paddy fields, up to their hocks in water. We were soon off again like fury to a Buddhist temple, where we left our desert boots and shoes at the doorstep before entering. Later we were on to a mob of performing elephants, before charging into a gem shop for the doctor to purchase a handful of star sapphires for his wife. I gathered his medical practice in the States must have been quite lucrative.

At the Galle Face, where we had dinner, I paid my share of the bill and we all agreed we had had a really good time and not a second had been wasted. As we parted, Dr Clough Frudenfeld gave me his card, with strict instructions to visit them when next in California. They were a wonderful couple, full of interest in everything. Our chance meeting had made a visit to Ceylon complete for us all, a fact we all realise as we very reluctantly went our own ways.

I knew I would like to have a chance to stay a lot longer on this most perfectly compact island, so crammed with its own wealth of products, both on and under the ground. I was standing on the side of the landing field—on which some rain had fallen during the night when my Comet 4 jet plane came in to land. Just after touch-down, a 'bird bath' of water in the middle of one set of wheels splashed up with such force that it buckled the underside of a wing flap, grounding the plane until repairs could be made. I, at least, was pleased at staying longer, even though the airline company might have been disappointed. However, a second plane was diverted and so we only had one extra night.

The new Comet took us in a south of easterly direction during the afternoon. I was on the four-hour flight to Singapore, where I felt I had to go in order to buy a duty-free slide projector. It had only cost £150 extra to allow me that privilege. Being about one degree of latitude to the north of the equator, the bus ride to the Embassy Hotel proved to be quite a warm one, although it was after dark by the time I'd ploughed through the customs gentlemen.

Following in the millions of footsteps of people with the same intention, I plunged into the Singapore markets to compare, haggle and finally buy some of the things I had in mind. The projector was the best and most automatic in the world, according to the Malayan shopkeeper. The transistor radios—which were also the

best in the world—came next, followed by binoculars, camera and
pens—also unsurpassed on this earth. They certainly were good,
and I was very pleased with my purchases, finishing with one of
the ultimate in watches, an Omega. This was for a present, so I
wound it up—and continued to wind it up for two hours—until
my finger showed signs of wear and tear but still it didn't seem to
be fully wound. The spring must have been half a mile long. I
called back into the shop from which I had purchased it, to ask
just how long it took to wind it up. I showed the Malayan
storekeeper my worn-out forefinger. He laughed until he was dark
brown in the face, after which he called all his friends, who also
rolled on the ground, coughing in spasms brought on by laughing.
I waited for this unusual show to come to an end, when the
shopkeeper managed to gasp out that it was a *self-winding watch*. He
added that if it was left stationary, a few turns by hand would have
fully wound it, after which the knob would free ratchet forever.

A little further along Change Alley—which I understood was
the name of the place I was in—a little man rushed up to me and
began to measure me with a tape. At first I thought he must have
been an undertaker, but he explained he was merely a tailor. He
would make me a suit from any material I chose in an hour or so.
I explained to him that I had been through this suit buying
business in London. To console him I bought a pair of socks
instead.

As I was standing looking in one of the few shops which
possessed a window, I heard a vaguely familiar sort of clicking
noise behind me. I knew this noise was made by high-heel shoes,
having been to Paris. Turning around, I saw a sight which took
my breath away. It was a Malayan girl, standing there smiling.
When my mouth finally snapped shut, all I could say to her was
that the stitches at the sides of her skirt seemed to be a bit weak,
and had come apart. She explained she had a *Cheong Sam*. I told
her that was nice for her, but that her skirt still needed mending.
Her olive-brown skin and vivid red lips accentuated the whiteness
of her teeth, as she laughed and thanked me. Blushing, I said:
'You're welcome.' I stumbled into the shop in a great hurry to buy
yet another ballpoint pen. I thought of this incident several years

later, when a doctor at Woomera informed me, as he packed up his instruments, that there was nothing wrong with my blood pressure.

That night at the Embassy a performer singing at a microphone was wearing another of those skirts with the weak stitches. As I sat in the cool on the open-air roof garden, I concluded that the cotton must have rotted due to the humidity.

The following night was spent in a plane flying over the equator. After stopping for petrol at Java, we came to the familiar shores of good old Australia in mid-morning and landed at Darwin. Everything suddenly seemed easy: I could read the posters on the walls, understand the voice coming from the loudspeakers. I could talk fluently to people, where nobody asked for francs, lire, drachmas or rupees. With the pleasure of being home, I phoned an old army friend living nearby, who sounded surprised when I told him who was calling. Knowing my usual place of abode, he asked me which desert I had just sprung from this time. When I told him 'the Sahara' he immediately hung up his receiver. He had always been on the watch for practical jokers.

Flying over Central Australia on the last lap, I looked down, wondering what poor unfortunate soul had to battle for a living in this desolate, harsh-looking country. On remembering, I came to the all too sudden realisation that it was me.